T0272793

Autobiography of Ma-Ka-Tai-Me-She-Kia-Kiak

Autobiography of Ma-Ka-Tai-Me-She-Kia-Kiak

Sauk Chief Black Hawk

MINT EDITIONS

Autobiography of Ma-Ka-Tai-Me-She-Kia-Kiak was first published in 1833.

This edition published by Mint Editions 2021.

ISBN 9781513135250 | E-ISBN 9781513295138

Published by Mint Editions®

MINT
EDITIONS

MintEditionBooks.com

Publishing Director: Jennifer Newens
Design & Production: Rachel Lopez Metzger
Project Manager: Micaela Clark
Typesetting: Westchester Publishing Services

Contents

Affidavit

Indian Agency,
Rock Island, October 16, 1833

I do hereby certify, that Makataimeshekiakiak, or Black Hawk, did call upon me, on his return to his people in August last, and expressed a great desire to have a History of his Life written and published, in order (as he said) "that the people of the United States, (among whom he had been traveling, and by whom he had been treated with great respect, friendship and hospitality,) might know the *causes* that had impelled him to act as he had done, and the *principles* by which he was governed."

In accordance with his request, I acted as Interpreter; and was particularly cautious to understand distinctly the narrative of Black Hawk throughout and have examined the work carefully since its completion, and have no hesitation in pronouncing it strictly correct, in all its particulars.

Given under my hand, at the Sac and Fox Agency, the day and date above written.

Antoine Le Clair,
V. S. Interpreter for the Sacs and Foxes

NE-KA-NA-WEN

MA-NE-SE-NO OKE-MAUT WAP-PI MA-QUAI

WA-TA-SAI WE-YEU,

Ai nan-ni ta co-si-ya-quai, na-katch ai she-ke she-he-nack, hai-me-ka-ti ya-quai ke-she-he-nack, ken-e-chawe-he-ke kai-pec-kien a-cob, ai-we-ne-she we-he-yen; ne-wai-ta-sa-mak ke-kosb-pe kai-a-poi qni-wat. No-ta-wach-pai pai-ke se-na-mon nan-ni-yoo, ai-ke-kai na-o-pen. Ni-me-to sai-ne-ni-wen, ne-ta-to-ta ken ai mo-he-man ta-ta-que, ne-me-to-sai-ne-ne-wen.

Nin-a-kai-ka poi-pon-ni chi-cha-yen, kai-ka-ya ha-ma-we pa-she-to-he-yen. Kai-na-ya kai-nen-ne-naip, he-nok ki-nok ke-cha-kai-ya, pai-no-yen ne-ket-te-sim-mak o-ke-te-wak ke-o-che, me-ka ti-ya-quois na-kach mai-qaoi, a-que-qui pa-che-qui ke-kan-ni ta-men-nin. Ke-to-ta we-yen, a-que-ka-ni-co-te she-tai-hai yen, nen, chai-cha-me-co kai-ke-me-se ai we-ke ken-ne-ta-mo-wat ken-na-wa-ha-o ma-co-qua-yeai-quoi. Ken-wen-na ak-che-man wen-ni-ta-hai ke-men-ne to-ta-we-yeu, ke-kog-hai ke-ta-shi ke-kai na-we-yen, he-na-cha wai-che-we to-mo-nan, ai pe-che-qua-chi mo-pen ma-me-co, mai-che-we-ta na-mo-nan, ne-ya-we-nan qui-a-ha-wa pe-ta-kek, a que-year tak-pa-she-qui a-to-ta-mo-wat, chi-ye-tuk he-ne cha-wai-chi he-ni-nan ke-o-chi-ta mow-ta-swee-pai che-qua-que.

He-ni-cha-hai poi-kai-nen na-na-so-si-yen, ai o-sa-ke-we-yen, ke-pe-me-kai-mi-kat hai-nen hac-yai na-na-co-si-peu, nen-a-kai-ne co-ten ne-co-ten ne-ka chi-a-quoi ne-me-cok me-to-sai ne-ne wak-kai ne-we-yen-nen, kai-shai ma-ni-to-ke ka-to-me-nak ke-wa-sai- he co-wai mi-a-me ka-chi pai-ko-tai-hear-pe kai-cee wa-wa kia he-pe ha-pe-nach-he-cha, na-na-ke-na-way ni-taain ai we-pa-he-wea to-to-na ca, ke-to-ta-we yeak, he-nok, mia-ni ai she-ke-ta ma-ke-si-yen, nen-a-kai na-co-ten ne-ka-he-nen e-ta-quois, wa-toi-na-ka che-ma-ke-keu na-ta-che tai-hai-ken ai mo-co-man ye-we-yeu ke-to-towe. E-nok ma-ni-hai she-ka-ta- ma

ka-si-yen, wen-e-cha-hai nai-ne-mak, mai-ko-ten ke ka-cha
ma-men-na-tuk we-yowe, keu-ke-nok ai she-me ma-na-ni
ta-men-ke-yowe.

MA-KA-TAI-ME-SHE -KIA-KIAK
Ma-taus-we Ki-sis, 1833

DEDICATION

(Translation)

To Brigadier General H. Atkinson:

Sir

The changes of fortune and vicissitudes of war made you my conqueror. When my last resources were exhausted, my warriors worn down with long and toilsome marches, we yielded, and I became your prisoner.

The story of my life is told in the following pages : it is intimately connected, and in some measure, identified with a part of the history of your own: I have, therefore, dedicated it to you.

The changes of many summers have brought old age upon me, and I cannot expect to survive many moons. Before I set out on my journey to the land of my fathers, I have determined to give my motives and reasons for my former hostilities to the whites, and to vindicate my character from misrepresentation. The kindness I received from you whilst a prisoner of war assures me that you will vouch for the facts contained in my narrative, so far as they came under your observation.

I am now an obscure member of a nation that formerly honored an respected my opinions. The pathway to glory is rough, and many gloomy hours obscure it. May the Great Spirit shed light on yours, and that you may never experience the humility that the power of the American government has reduced me to, is the wish of him, who, in his native forests, was once as proud and bold as yourself.

BLACK HAWK
10th Moon, 1833

The Life of Black Hawk

I was born at the Sac village, on Rock river, in the year 1767, and am now in my 67th year. My great grandfather, Nanamakee, or Thunder, according to the tradition given me by my father, Pyesa, was born in the vicinity of Montreal, Canada, where the Great Spirit first placed the Sac nation, and inspired him with a belief that, at the end of four years he should see a *white man*, who would be to him a father. Consequently he blacked his face, and eat but once a day, just as the sun was going down, for three years, and continued dreaming, throughout all this time whenever he slept. When the Great Spirit again appeared to him, and told him that, at the end of one year more, he should meet his father, and directed him to start seven days before its expiration, and take with him his two brothers, Namah, or Sturgeon, and Paukahummawa, or Sunfish, and travel in a direction to the left of sun-rising. After pursuing this course for five days, he sent out his two brothers to listen if they could hear a noise, and if so, to fasten some grass to the end of a pole, erect it, pointing in the direction of the sound, and then return to him.

Early next morning they returned, and reported that they had heard sounds which appeared near at hand, and that they had fulfilled his order. They all then started for the place where the pole had been erected; when, on reaching it, Nanamakee left his party and went alone to the place from whence the sounds proceeded, and found, that the white man had arrived and pitched his tent. When he came in sight, his father came out to meet him. He took him by the hand and welcomed him into his tent. He told him that he was the son of the King of France; that he had been dreaming for four years; that the Great Spirit had directed him to come here, where he should meet a nation of people who had never yet seen a white man; that they should be his children and he should be their father; that he had communicated these things to the King, his father, who laughed at him and called him Mashena, but he insisted on coming here to meet his children where the Great Spirit had directed him. The king had told him that he would find neither land nor people; that this was an uninhabited region of lakes and mountains, but, finding that he would have no peace without it, he fitted out a napequa, manned it, and gave him charge of it, when he immediately loaded it, set sail and had now landed on the very day that the Great Spirit had told him in his dreams he should meet his children. He had now met the man who should, in future, have charge of all the nation.

He then presented him with a medal which he hung round his neck. Nanamakee informed him of his dreaming, and told him that his two brothers remained a little way behind. His father gave him a shirt, a blanket and a handkerchief besides a variety of other presents, and told him to go and bring his brethren. Having laid aside his buffalo robe and dressed himself in his new dress, he started to meet his brothers. When they met he explained to them his meeting with the white man and exhibited to their view the presents that had made him. He then took off his medal and placed it on his elder brother Namah, and requested them both to go with him to his father.

They proceeded thither, were where ushered into the tent, and after some brief ceremony his father opened a chest and took presents therefrom for the new comers. He discovered that Nanamakee had given his medal to his elder brother Namah. He told him that he had done wrong; that he should wear that medal himself, as he had others for his brothers. That which he had given him was typical of the rank he should hold in the nation; that his brothers could only rank as *civil chiefs*, and that their duties should consist of taking care of the village and attending to its civil concerns, whilst his rank, from his superior knowledge, placed him over all. If the nation should get into any difficulty with another, then his puccohawama, or sovereign decree, must be obeyed. If he declared war he must lead them on to battle; that the Great Spirit had made him a great and brave general, and had sent him here to give him that medal and make presents to him for his people.

His father remained four days, during which time he gave him guns, powder and lead, spears and lances, and taught him their use, so that in war he might be able to chastise his enemies, and in peace they could kill buffalo, deer and other game necessary for the comforts and luxuries of life. He then presented the others with various kinds of cooking utensils and taught them their uses. After having given them large quantities of goods as presents, and everything necessary for their comfort, he set sail for France, promising to meet them again, at the same place, after the 12th moon.

The three newly made chiefs returned to their village and explained to Mukataquet, their father, who was the principal chief of the nation, what had been said and done.

The old chief had some dogs killed and made a feast preparatory to resigning his scepter, to which all the nation were invited. Great anxiety prevailed among them to know what the three brothers had seen and heard. When the old chief arose and related to them the sayings and doings of his three sons, and concluded by saying that the Great Spirit had directed that these, his three sons, should take the rank and power that had once been his, and that he yielded these honors and duties willingly to them, because it was the wish of the Great Spirit, and he could never consent to make him angry.

He now presented the great medicine bag to Nanamakee, and told him that he "cheerfully resigned it to him, it is the soul of our nation, it has never yet been disgraced and I will expect you to keep it unsullied."

Some dissensions arose among them, in consequence of so much power being given to Nanamakee, he being so young a man. To quiet them, Nanamakee, during a violent thunder storm, told them that he had caused it, and that it was an exemplification of the name the Great Spirit had given him. During the storm the lightning struck, and set fire to a tree near by, a sight they had never witnessed before. He went to it and brought away some of its burning branches, made a fire in the lodge and seated his brothers around it opposite to one another, while he stood up and addressed his people as follows:

"I am yet young, but the Great Spirit has called me to the rank I hold among you. I have never sought to be more than my birth entitled me to. I have not been ambitious, nor was it ever my wish while my father was yet among the living to take his place, nor have I now usurped his powers. The Great Spirit caused me to dream for four years. He told me where to go and meet the white man who would be a kind father to us all. I obeyed. I went, and have seen and know our new father.

"You have all heard what was said and done. The Great Spirit directed him to come and meet me, and it is his order that places me at the head of my nation, the place which my father has willingly resigned.

"You have all witnessed the power that has been given me by the Great Spirit, in making that fire, and all that I now ask is that these, my two chiefs, may never let it go out. That they may preserve peace among you and administer to the wants of the needy. And should an enemy invade our country, I will then, and not until then, assume command, and go forth with my band of brave warriors and endeavor to chastise them."

At the conclusion of this speech every voice cried out for Nanamakee. All were satisfied when they found that the Great Spirit had done what they had suspected was the work of Nanamakee, he being a very shrewd young man.

The next spring according to promise their French father returned, with his napequa richly laden with goods, which were distributed among them. He continued for a long time to keep up a regular trade with them, they giving him in exchange for his goods furs and peltries.

After a long time the British overpowered the French, the two nations being at War, and drove them away from Quebec, taking possession of it themselves. The different tribes of Indians around our nation, envying our people, united their forces against them and by their combined strength succeeded in driving them to Montreal, and from thence to Mackinac. Here our people first met our British father, who furnished them with goods. Their enemies still wantonly pursued them and drove them to different places along the lake. At last they made a village near Green Bay, on what is now called Sac river, having derived its name from this circumstance. Here they held a council with the Foxes, and a national treaty of friendship and alliance was agreed upon. The Foxes abandoned their village and joined the Sacs. This arrangement, being mutually obligatory upon both parties, as neither were sufficiently strong to meet their enemies with any hope of success, they soon became as one band or nation of people. They were driven, however, by the combined forces of their enemies to the Wisconsin. They remained here for sometime, until a party of their young men, who descended Rock river to its mouth, had returned and made a favorable report of the country. They all descended Rock river, drove the Kaskaskias from the country and commenced the erection of their village, determined never to leave it.

At this village I was born, being a lineal descendant of the first chief, Nanamakee, or Thunder. Few, if any events of note transpired within my recollection until about my fifteenth year. I was not allowed to paint or wear feathers, but distinguished myself at an early age by wounding an enemy; consequently I was placed in the ranks of the Braves.

Soon after this a leading chief of the Muscow nation came to our village for recruits to go to war against the Osages, our common enemy.

I volunteered my services to go, as my father had joined him, and was proud to have an opportunity to prove to him that I was not an unworthy son, and that I had courage and bravery. It was not long before we met the enemy and a battle immediately ensued. Standing by my father's side, I saw him kill his antagonist and tear the scalp from off his head. Fired with valor and ambition, I rushed furiously upon another and smote him to the earth with my tomahawk. I then ran my lance through his body, took off his scalp and returned in triumph to my father. He said nothing but looked well pleased. This was the first man I killed. The enemy's loss in this engagement having been very great, they immediately retreated, which put an end to the war for the time being. Our party then returned to the village and danced over the scalps we had taken. This was the first time I was permitted to join in a scalp dance.

After a few moons had passed, being acquired considerable reputation as a brave, I led a party of seven and attacked one hundred Osages! I killed one man and left him for my comrades to scalp while I was taking observations of the strength and preparations of the enemy. Finding that they were equally well armed with ourselves, I ordered a retreat and came off without the loss of a man. This excursion gained for me great applause, and enabled me, before a great while, to raise a party of one hundred and eighty to march against the Osages. We left our village in high spirits and marched over a rugged country, until we reached the land of the Osages, on the borders of the Missouri.

We followed their trail until we arrived at the village, which we approached with exceeding caution, thinking that they were all here, but found, to our sorrow, that they had deserted it. The party became dissatisfied in consequence of this disappointment, and all, with the exception of five noble braves, dispensed and went home. I then placed myself at the head of this brave little band, and thanked the Great Spirit that so *many* had remained. We took to the trail of our enemies, with a full determination never to return without some trophy of victory. We followed cautiously on for several days, killed one man and a boy, and returned home with their scalps.

In consequence of this mutiny in camp, I was not again able to raise a sufficient force to go against the Osages until about my Nineteenth year. During this interim they committed many outrages on our nation; hence I succeeded in recruiting two hundred efficient warriors, and early one morning took up the line of march. In a few days we were in the enemy's country, and we had not gone far before we met a force equal to our own with which to contend. A general battle immediately commenced, although my warriors were considerably fatigued by forced marches. Each party fought desperately. The enemy seemed unwilling to yield the ground and we were determined to conquer or die. A great number of Osages were killed and many wounded before they commenced a retreat. A band of warriors more brave, skillful and efficient than mine could not be found. In this engagement I killed five men and one squaw, and had the good fortune to take the scalps of all I struck with one exception—that of the squaw, who was accidentally killed. The enemy's loss in this engagement was about one hundred braves. Ours nineteen. We then returned to our village well pleased with our success, and danced over the scalps which we had taken.

The Osages, in consequence of their great loss in this battle, became satisfied to remain on their own lands. This stopped for a while their depredations on our nation. Our attention was now directed towards an ancient enemy who had decoyed and murdered some of our helpless women and children. I started with my father, who took command of a small party, and proceeded against the enemy to chastise them for the wrongs they had heaped upon us. We met near the Merimac and an action ensued; the Cherokees having a great advantage in point of numbers. Early in this engagement my father was wounded in the thigh, but succeeded in killing his enemy before he fell. Seeing that he had fallen, I assumed command, and fought desperately until the enemy commenced retreating before the well directed blows of our braves. I returned to my father to administer to his necessities, but nothing could be done for him. The medicine man said the wound was mortal, from which he soon after died. In this battle I killed three men and wounded several. The enemy's loss was twenty-eight and ours seven.

I now fell heir to the great medicine bag of my forefathers, which had belonged to my father. I took it, buried our dead, and returned with my party, sad and sorrowful, to our village, in consequence of the loss of my father.

Owing to this misfortune I blacked my face, fasted and prayed to the Great Spirit for five years, during which time I remained in a civil capacity, hunting and fishing.

The Osages having again commenced aggressions on our people, and the Great Spirit having taken pity on me, I took a small party and went against them. I could only find six of them, and their forces being so weak, I thought it would be cowardly to kill them, but took them prisoners and carried them to our Spanish father at St. Louis, gave them up to him and then returned to our village.

Determined on the final and complete extermination of the dastardly Osages, in punishment for the injuries our people had received from them, I commenced recruiting a strong force, immediately on my return, and stated in the third moon, with five hundred Sacs and Foxes, and one hundred Iowas, and marched against the enemy. We continued our march for many days before we came upon their trail, which was discovered late in the day. We encamped for the night, made an early start next morning, and before sundown we fell upon forty lodges, killed all the inhabitants except two squaws, whom I took as prisoners. Doing this engagement I killed seven men and two boys with my own hands. In this battle many of the bravest warriors among the Osages were killed, which caused those who yet remained of their nation to keep within the boundaries of their own land and cease their aggressions upon our hunting grounds.

The loss of my father, by the Cherokees, made me anxious to avenge his death by the utter annihilation, if possible, of the last remnant of their tribe. I accordingly commenced collecting another party to go against them. Having succeeded in this, I started with my braves and went into their country, but I found only five of their people, whom I took prisoners. I afterwards released four of them, the other, a young squaw, we brought home. Great as was my hatred of these people, I could not kill so small a party.

About the close of the ninth moon, I led a large party against the Chippewas, Kaskaskias and Osages. This was the commencement of a long and arduous campaign, which terminated in my thirty-fifth year, after having had seven regular engagements and numerous small skirmishes. During this campaign several hundred of the enemy were slain. I killed thirteen of their bravest warriors with my own hands.

Our enemies having now been driven from our hunting grounds, with so great a loss as they sustained, we returned in peace to our village. After the seasons of mourning and burying our dead braves and of feasting and dancing had passed, we commenced preparations for our winter's hunt. When all was ready we started on the chase and returned richly laden with the fruits of the hunter's toil.

We usually paid a visit to St. Louis every summer, but in consequence of the long protracted war in which we had been engaged, I had not been there for some years.

Our difficulties all having been settled, I concluded to take a small party and go down to see our Spanish father during the summer. We went, and on our arrival put up our lodges where the market house now stands. After painting and dressing we called to see our Spanish father and were kindly received. He gave us a great variety of presents and an abundance of provisions. We danced through the town as usual, and the inhabitants all seemed well pleased. They seemed to us like brothers, and always gave us good advice. On my next and last visit to our Spanish father, I discovered on landing, that all was not right. Every countenance seemed sad and gloomy. I inquired the cause and was informed that the Americans were coming to take possession of the town and country, and that we were to lose our Spanish father. This news made me and my band exceedingly sad, because we had always heard bad accounts of the Americans from the Indians who had lived near them. We were very sorry to lose our Spanish father, who had always treated us with great friendship.

A few days afterwards the Americans arrived. I, in company with my band, went to take leave for the last time of our father. The Americans came to see him also. Seeing their approach, we passed out at one door as they came in at another. We immediately embarked in our canoes for our village on Rock river, not liking the change anymore than our friends at St. Louis appeared to.

On arriving at our village we gave out the news that a strange people had taken possession of St. Louis and that we should never see our generous Spanish father again. This information cast a deep gloom over our people.

Sometime afterwards a boat came up the river with a young American chief, at that time Lieutenant, and afterwards General Pike, and a small party of soldiers aboard. The boat at length arrived at Rock river and the young chief came on shore with his interpreter. He made us a speech and gave us some presents, in return for which we gave him meat and such other provisions as we could spare.

We were well pleased with the speech of the young chief. He gave us good advice and said our American father would treat us well. He presented us an American flag which we hoisted. He then requested us to lower the *British colors*, which were waving in the air, and to give him our British medals, promising to send others on his return to St. Louis. This we declined to do as we wished to have two fathers.

When the young chief started we sent runners to the village of the Foxes, some miles distant, to direct them to treat him well as he passed, which they did. He went to the head of the Mississippi and then returned to St. Louis. We did not see any Americans again for sometime, being supplied with goods by British traders.

We were fortunate in not giving up our medals, for we learned afterwards, from our traders, that the chiefs high up the Mississippi, who gave theirs, never received any in exchange for them. But the fault was not with the young American chief. He was a good man, a great brave, and I have since learned, died in his country's service.

Some moons after this young chief had descended the Mississippi, one of our people killed an American, was taken prisoner and was confined in the prison at St. Louis for the offence. We held a council at our village to see what could be done for him, and determined that Quashquame, Pashepaho, Ouchequaka and Hashequarhiqua should go down to St. Louis, see our American father and do all they could to have our friend released by paying for the person killed, thus covering the blood and satisfying the relations of the murdered man. This being the only means with us for saving a person who had killed another, and we then thought it was the same way with the whites.

The party started with the good wishes of the whole nation, who had high hopes that the emissaries would accomplish the object of their mission. The relations of the prisoner blacked their faces and fasted, hoping the Great Spirit would take pity on them and return husband and father to his sorrowing wife and weeping children.

Quashquame and party remained a long time absent. They at length returned and encamped near the village, a short distance below it, and did not come up that day, nor did anyone approach their camp. They appeared to be dressed in fine coats and had medals. From these circumstances we were in hopes that they had brought good news. Early the next morning the Council Lodge was crowded, Quashquame and party came up and gave us the following account of their mission:

On our arrival at St. Louis we met our American father and explained to him our business, urging the release of our friend. The American chief told us he wanted land. We agreed to give him some on the west side of the Mississippi, likewise more on the Illinois side opposite Jeffreon. When the business was all arranged we expected to have our friend released to come home with us. About the time we were ready to start our brother was let out of the prison. He started and ran a short distance when he was SHOT DEAD!

This was all they could remember of what had been said and done. It subsequently appeared that they had been drunk the greater part of the time while at St. Louis.

This was all myself and nation knew of the treaty of 1804. It has since been explained to me. I found by that treaty, that all of the country east of the Mississippi, and south of Jeffreon was ceded to the United States for one thousand dollars a year. I will leave it to the people of the United States to say whether our nation was properly represented in this treaty? Or whether we received a fair compensation for the extent of country ceded by these four individuals?

I could say much more respecting this treaty, but I will not at this time. It has been the origin of all our serious difficulties with the whites.

Sometime after this treaty was made, a war chief with a party of soldiers came up in keel boats, encamped a short distance above the head of the Des Moines rapids, and commenced cutting timber and building houses. The news of their arrival was soon carried to all our villages, to confer upon which many councils were held. We could not understand the intention, or comprehend the reason why the Americans wanted to build homes at that place. We were told that they were a party of soldiers, who had brought great guns with them, and looked like a war party of whites.

A number of people immediately went down to see what was going on, myself among them. On our arrival we found that they were building a fort. The soldiers were busily engaged in cutting timber, and I observed that they took their arms with them when they went to the woods. The whole party acted as they would do in an enemy's country. The chiefs held a council with the officers, or head men of the party, which I did not attend, but understood from them that the war chief had said that they were building homes for a trader who was coming there to live, and would sell us goods very cheap, and that the soldiers were to remain to keep him company. We were pleased at this information ad hoped that it was all true, but we were not so credulous as to believe that all these buildings were intended merely for the accommodation of a trader. Being distrustful of their intentions, we were anxious for them to leave off building and go back down the river.

By this time a considerable number of Indians had arrived to see what was doing. I discovered that the whites were alarmed. Some of our young men watched a party of soldiers, who went out to work, carrying their arms, which were laid aside before they commenced. Having stolen quietly to the spot they seized the guns and gave a wild yell! The party threw down their axes and ran for their arms, but found them gone, and themselves surrounded. Our young men laughed at them and returned their weapons.

When this party came to the fort they reported what had been done, and the war chief made a serious affair of it. He called our chiefs to council inside his fort. This created considerable excitement in our camp, everyone wanting to know what was going to be done. The picketing which had been put up, being low, every Indian crowded around the fort, got upon blocks of wood and old barrels that they might see what was going on inside. Some were armed with guns and others with bows and arrows. We used this precaution, seeing that the soldiers had their guns loaded and having seen them load their big guns in the morning.

A party of our braves commenced dancing and proceeded up to the gate with the intention of, going in, but were stopped. The council immediately broke up, the soldiers with their guns in hands rushed out from the rooms where they had been concealed. The cannon were hauled to the gateway, and a soldier came running with fire in his hand, ready to apply the match. Our braves gave way and retired to the camp. There was no preconcerted plan to attack the whites at that time, but I am of the opinion now that had our braves got into the fort all of the whites would have been killed, as were the British soldiers at Mackinac many years before.

We broke up our camp and returned to Rock river. A short time afterward the party at the fort received reinforcements, among whom we observed some of our old friends from St. Louis.

Soon after our return from Fort Madison runners came to our village from the Shawnee Prophet. Others were despatched by him to the village of the Winnebagoes, with invitations for us to meet him on the Wabash. Accordingly a party went from each village.

All of our party returned, among whom came a prophet, who explained to us the bad treatment the different nations of Indians had received from the Americans, by giving them a few presents and taking their land from them.

I remember well his saying: "If you do not join your friends on the Wabash, the Americans will take this very village from you!" I little thought then that his words would come true, supposing that he used these arguments merely to encourage us to join him, which we concluded not to do. He then returned to the Wabash, where a party of Winnebagoes had preceded him, and preparations were making for war. A battle soon ensued in which several Winnebagoes were killed. As soon as their nation heard of this battle, and that some of their people had been killed, they sent several war parties in different directions. One to the mining county, one to Prairie du Chien, and another to Fort Madison. The latter returned by our village and exhibited several scalps which they had taken. Their success induced several parties to go against the fort. Myself and several of my band joined the last party, and were determined to take the fort. We arrived in the vicinity during the night. The spies that we had sent out several days before to watch the movements of those at the garrison, and ascertain their numbers, came to us and gave the following information: "A keel arrived from below this evening with seventeen men. There are about fifty men in the fort and they march out every morning to exercise." It was immediately determined that we should conceal ourselves in a position as near as practicable to where the soldiers should come out, and when the signal was given each one was to fire on them and rush into the fort. With my knife I dug a hole in the ground deep enough that by placing a few weeds around it, succeeded in concealing myself. I was so near the fort that I could hear the sentinels walking on their beats. By day break I had finished my work and was anxiously awaiting the rising of the sun. The morning drum beat. I examined the priming of my gun, and eagerly watched for the gate to open. It did open, but instead of the troops, a young man came out alone and the gate closed after him. He passed so close to me that I could have killed him with my knife, but I let him pass unharmed. He kept the path toward the river, and had he gone one step from it, he must have come upon us and would have been killed. He returned immediately and entered the gate. I would now have rushed for the gate and entered it with him, but I feared that our party was not prepared to follow me.

The gate opened again when four men emerged and went down to the river for wood. While they were gone another man came out, walked toward the river, was fired on and killed by a Winnebago. The others started and ran rapidly towards the fort, but two of them were shot down dead. We then took shelter under the river's bank out of reach of the firing from the fort.

The firing now commenced from both parties and was kept up without cessation all day. I advised our party to set fire to the fort, and commenced preparing arrows for that purpose. At night we made the attempt, and succeeded in firing the buildings several times, but without effect, as the fire was always instantly extinguished.

The next day I took my rifle and shot in two the cord by which they hoisted their flag, and prevented them from raising it again. We continued firing until our ammunition was expended. Finding that we could not take the fort, we returned home, having one Winnebago killed and one wounded during the siege.

I have since learned that the trader who lived in the fort, wounded the Winnebago while he was scalping the first man that was killed. The Winnebago recovered, and is now living, and is very friendly disposed towards the trader, believing him to be a great brave.

Soon after our return home, news reached us that a war was going to take place between the British and the Americans.

Runners continued to arrive from different tribes, all confirming the reports of the expected war. The British agent, Colonel Dixon, was holding talks with, and making presents to the different tribes. I had not made up my mind whether to join the British or remain neutral. I had not discovered yet one good trait in the character of the Americans who had come to the country. They made fair promises but never fulfilled them, while the British made but few, and we could always rely implicitly on their word.

One of our people having killed a Frenchman at Prairie du Chien, the British took him prisoner and said they would shoot him next day. His family were encamped a short distance below the mouth of the Wisconsin. He begged for permission to go and see them that night, as he was to die the next day. They permitted him to go after he had promised them to return by sunrise the next morning.

He visited his family, which consisted of his wife and six children. I can not describe their meeting and parting so as to be understood by the whites, as it appears that their feelings are acted upon by certain rules laid down by their preachers, while ours are governed by the monitor within us. He bade his loved ones the last sad farewell and hurried across the prairie to the fort and arrived in time. The soldiers were ready and immediately marched out and shot him down. I visited the stricken family, and by hunting and fishing provided for them until they reached their relations.

Why did the Great Spirit ever send the whites to this island to drive us from our homes and introduce among us poisonous liquors, disease and death? They should have remained in the land the Great Spirit allotted them. But I will proceed with my story. My memory, however, is not very good since my late visit to the white people. I have still a buzzing noise in my ear from the noise and bustle incident to travel. I may give some parts of my story out of place, but will make my best endeavors to be correct.

Several of our chiefs were called upon to go to Washington to see our Great Father. They started and during their absence I went to Peoria, on the Illinois river, to see an old friend and get his advice. He was a man who always told u the truth, sad knew everything that was going on. When I arrived at Peoria he had gone to Chicago, and was not at home. I visited the Pottawattomie villages and then returned to Rock river. Soon after which our friends returned from their visit to the Great Father and reported what had been said and done. Their Great Father told them that in the event of a war taking place with England, not to interfere on either side, but remain neutral. He did not want our help, but wished us to hunt and supply our families, and remain in peace. He said that British traders would not be allowed to come on the Mississippi to furnish us with goods, but that we would be well supplied by an American trader. Our chiefs then told him that the British traders always gave us credit in the fall for guns, powder and goods, to enable us to hunt and clothe our families. He replied that the trader at Fort Madison would have plenty of goods, and if we should go there in the autumn of the year, he would supply us on credit, as the British traders had done. The party gave a good account of what they had seen and the kind treatment they had received. This information pleased us all very much. We all agreed to follow our Great Father's advice and not interfere in the war. Our women were much pleased at the good news. Everything went on cheerfully in our village. We resumed our pastimes of playing ball, horse-racing and dancing, which had been laid aside when this great war was first talked about. We had fine crops of corn which were now ripe, and our women were busily engaged in gathering it and making caches to contain it.

In a short time we were ready to start to Fort Madison to get our supply of goods, that we might proceed to our hunting grounds. We passed merrily down the river, all in high spirits. I had determined to spend the winter at my old favorite hunting ground on Skunk river. I left part of my corn and mats at its mouth to take up as we returned and many others did the same.

The next morning we arrived at the fort and made our encampment. Myself and principal men paid a visit to the war chief at the fort. He received us kindly and gave us some tobacco, pipes and provisions.

The trader came in and we all shook hands with him, for on him all our dependence was placed, to enable us to hunt and thereby support our families. We waited a long time, expecting the trader would tell us

SAUK CHIEF BLACK HAWK

that he had orders from our Great Father to supply us with goods, but he said nothing on the subject. I got up and told him in a short speech what we had come for, and hoped he had plenty of goods to supply us. I told him that he should be well paid in the spring, and concluded by informing him that we had decided to follow our Great Father's advice and not go to war.

He said that he was happy to hear that we had concluded to remain in peace. That he had a large quantity of goods, and that if we had made a good hunt we should be well supplied, but he remarked that he had received no instructions to furnish us anything on credit, nor could he give us any without receiving the pay for them on the spot!

We informed him what our Great Father had told our chiefs at Washington, and contended that he could supply us if he would, believing that our Great Father always spoke the truth. The war chief said the trader could not furnish us on credit, and that he had received no instructions from our Great Father at Washington. We left the fort dissatisfied and went to camp. What was now to be done we knew not. We questioned the party that brought us the news from our Great Father, that we could get credit for our winter supplies at this place. They still told the same story and insisted on its truth. Few of us slept that night. All was gloom and discontent.

In the morning a canoe was seen descending the river, bearing an express, who brought intelligence that La Gutrie, a British trader, had landed at Rock Island with two boat loads of goods. He requested us to come up immediately as he had good news for us, and a variety of presents. The express presented us with tobacco, pipes and wampum. The news ran through our camp like fire through dry grass on the prairie. Our lodges were soon taken down and we all started for Rock Island. Here ended all hopes of our remaining at peace, having been forced into war by being deceived.

Our party were not long in getting to Rock Island. When we came in sight and saw tents pitched, we yelled, fired our guns and beat our drums. Guns were immediately fired at the island, returning our salute, and a British flag hoisted. We loaded, were cordially received by La Gutrie, and then smoked the pipe with him. After which he made a speech to us, saying that he had been sent by Col. Dixon. He gave us a number of handsome presents, among them a large silk flag and a keg of rum. He then told us to retire, take some refreshments and rest ourselves, as he would have more to say to us next day.

We accordingly retired to our lodges, which in the meantime had been put up, and spent the night. The next morning we called upon him and told him we wanted his two boat loads of goods to divide among our people, for which he should be well paid in the spring in furs and peltries. He consented for us to take them and do as we pleased with them. While our people were dividing the goods, he took me aside and informed me that Colonel Dixon was at Green Bay with twelve boats loaded with goods, guns and ammunition. He wished to raise a party immediately and go to him. He said our friend, the trader at Peoria, was collecting the Pottawattomies and would be there before us. I communicated this information to my braves, and a party of two hundred warriors were soon collected and ready to depart. I paid a visit to the lodge of an old friend, who had been the comrade of my youth, and had been in many war parties with me, but was now crippled and no longer able to travel. He had a son that I had adopted as my own, and who had hunted with me the two winters preceding. I wished my old friend to let him go with me. He objected, saying he could not get his support if he did attend me, and that I, who had always provided for him since his misfortune, would be gone, therefore he could not spare him as he had no other dependence. I offered to leave my son in his stead but he refused to give his consent. He said that he did not like the war, as he had been down the river and had been well treated by the Americans and could not fight against them. He had promised to winter near a white settler above Salt river, and must take his son with him. We parted and I soon concluded my arrangements and started with my party for Green Bay. On our arrival there we found a large encampment; were well received by Colonel Dixon and the war chiefs who were with him. He gave us plenty of provisions, tobacco and pipes, saying that he would hold a council with us the next day. In the encampment I found a great number of Kickapoos, Ottawas and Winnebagoes. I visited all their camps and found them in high spirits. They had all received new guns, ammunition and a variety of clothing.

In the evening a messenger came to visit Colonel Dixon. I went to his tent, in which them were two other war chiefs and an interpreter. He received me with a hearty shake of the hand; presented me to the other chiefs, who treated me cordially, expressing themselves as being much. Pleased to meet me. After I was seated Colonel Dixon said: "General Black Hawk, I sent for you to explain to you what we are going to do and give you the reasons for our coming here. Our friend,

La Gutrie, informs us in the letter you brought from him, of what has lately taken place. You will now have to hold us fast by the hand. Your English Father has found out that the Americans want to take your country from you and has sent me and my braves to drive them back to their own country. He has, likewise, sent a large quantity of arms and ammunition, and we want all your warriors to join us."

He then placed a medal around my neck and gave me a paper, which I lost in the late war, and a silk flag, saying: "You are to command all the braves that will leave here the day after tomorrow, to join our braves at Detroit."

I told him I was very much disappointed, as I wanted to descend the Mississippi and make war upon the settlements. He said he had been ordered to lay in waste the country around St. Louis. But having been a trader on the Mississippi for many years himself, and always having been treated kindly by the people there, he could not send brave men to murder helpless women and innocent children. There were no soldiers there for us to fight, and where he was going to send us there were a great many of them. If we defeated them the Mississippi country should be ours. I was much pleased with this speech, as it was spoken by a brave.

I inquired about my old friend, the trader at Peoria, and observed, "that I had expected that he would have been here before me." He shook his head and said, "I have sent express after express for him, and have offered him great sums of money to come and bring the Pottawatomies and Kickapoos with him." He refused, saying, "Your British father has not enough money to induce me to join you. I have now laid a trap for him. I have sent Gomo and a party of Indians to take him prisoner and bring him here alive. I expect him in a few days."

The next day arms and ammunition, knives, tomahawks and clothing were given to my band. We had a great feast in the evening, and the morning following I started with about five hundred braves to join the British army. We passed Chicago and observed that the fort had been evacuated by the Americans, and their soldiers had gone to Fort Wayne. They were attacked a short distance from the fort and defeated. They had a considerable quantity of powder in the fort at Chicago, which they had promised to the Indians, but the night before they marched away they destroyed it by throwing it into a well. If they had fulfilled their word to the Indians, they doubtless would have gone to Fort Wayne without molestation. On our arrival, I found that the

Indians had several prisoners, and I advised them to treat them well. We continued our march, joining the British below Detroit, soon after which we had a battle. The Americans fought well, and drove us back with considerable loss. I was greatly surprised at this, as I had been told that the Americans would not fight.

Our next movement was against a fortified place. I was stationed with my braves to prevent any person going to, or coming from the fort. I found two men taking care of cattle and took them prisoners. I would not kill them, but delivered them to the British war chief. Soon after, several boats came down the river fail of American soldiers. They landed on the opposite side, took the British batteries, and pursued the soldiers that had left them. They went too far without knowing the strength of the British and were defeated. I hurried across the river, anxious for an opportunity to show the courage of my braves, but before we reached the scene of battle all was over.

The British had taken many prisoners and the Indians were killing them. I immediately put a stop to it, as I never thought it brave, but base and cowardly to kill in unarmed and helpless foe. We remained here for sometime. I can not detail what took place, as I was stationed with my braves in the woods. It appeared, however, that the British could not take this fort, for we marched to another, some distance off. When we approached it, I found a small stockade, and concluded that there were not many men in it. The British war chief sent a flag of truce. Colonel Dixon carried it, but soon returned, reporting that the young war chief in command would not give up the fort without fighting. Colonel Dixon came to me and said, "you will see tomorrow, how easily we will take that fort." I was of the same opinion, but when the morning came I was disappointed. The British advanced and commenced the attack, fighting like true braves, but were defeated by the braves in the fort, and a great number of our men were killed. The British army was making preparations to retreat. I was now tired of being with them, our success being bad, and having got no plunder. I determined on leaving them and returning to Rock river, to see what had become of my wife and children, as I had not heard from them since I left home. That night I took about twenty of my braves, and left the British camp for home. On our journey we met no one until we came to the Illinois river. Here we found two lodges of Pottawattomies. They received us in a very friendly manner, and gave us something to eat. I inquired about their friends who were with the British. They said there had been some fighting on the Illinois river, and that my friend, the Peoria trader, had been taken prisoner. "By Gomo and his party?" I immediately inquired. They replied, "no, but by the Americans, who came up with boats. They took him and the French settlers prisoners, and they burned the village of Peoria." They could give us no information regarding our friends on Rock river. In three days more we were in the vicinity of our village, and were soon after surprised to find that a party of Americans had followed us from the British camp. One of them, more daring than his comrades, had made his way through the thicket on foot, and was just in the act of shooting me when I discovered him. I then ordered him to surrender, marched him into camp, and turned him over to a number of our young men with this injunction: "Treat him as a brother, as I have concluded to adopt him in our tribe."

A little while before this occurrence I had directed my party to proceed to the village, as I had discovered a smoke ascending from a hollow in the bluff, and wished to go alone to the place from whence the smoke proceeded, to see who was there. I approached the spot, and when I came in view of the fire, I saw an old man sitting in sorrow beneath a mat which he had stretched over him. At any other time I would have turned away without disturbing him, knowing that he came here to be alone, to humble himself before the Great Spirit, that he might take pity on him. I approached and seated myself beside him. He gave one look at me and then fixed his eyes on the ground. It was my old friend. I anxiously inquired for his son, my adopted child, and what had befallen our people. My old comrade seemed scarcely alive. He must have fasted a long time. I lighted my pipe and put it into his mouth. He eagerly drew a few puffs, cast up his eyes which met mine, and recognized me. His eyes were glassy and he would again have fallen into forgetfulness, had I not given him some water, which revived him. I again inquired, "what has befallen our people, and what has become of our son?"

In a feeble voice he said, "Soon after your departure to join the British, I descended the river with a small party, to winter at the place I told you the white man had asked me to come to. When we arrived I found that a fort had been built, and the white family that had invited me to come and hunt near them had removed to it. I then paid a visit to the fort to tell the white people that my little band were friendly, and that we wished to hunt in the vicinity of the fort. The war chief who commanded there, told me that we might hunt on the Illinois side of the Mississippi, and no person would trouble us. That the horsemen only ranged on the Missouri side, and he had directed them not to cross the river. I was pleased with this assurance of safety, and immediately crossed over and made my winter's camp. Game was plenty. We lived happy, and often talked of you. My boy regretted your absence and the hardships you would have to undergo. We had been here about two moons, when my boy went out as usual to hunt. Night came on and he did not return. I was alarmed for his safety and passed a sleepless night. In the morning my old woman went to the other lodges and gave the alarm and all turned out to hunt for the missing one. There being snow upon the ground they soon came upon his track, and after pursuing it for some distance, found he was on the trail of a deer, which led toward the river. They soon came to the place where he had stood and fired, and near by, hanging on the branch of a tree, found the deer, which he had killed and skinned. But here were also found the tracks of white men. They had taken my boy prisoner. Their tracks led across the river and then down towards the fort. My friends followed on the trail, and soon found my boy lying dead. He had been most cruelly murdered. His face was shot to pieces, his body stabbed in several places and his head scalped. His arms were pinioned behind him."

The old man paused for sometime, and then told me that his wife had died on their way up the Mississippi. I took the hand of my old friend in mine and pledged myself to avenge the death of his son. It was now dark, and a terrible storm was raging. The rain was descending in heavy torrents, the thunder was rolling in the heavens, and the lightning flashed athwart the sky. I had taken my blanket off and wrapped it around the feeble old man. When the storm abated I kindled a fire and took hold of my old friend to remove him nearer to it. He was dead! I remained with him during the night. Some of my party came early in the morning to look for me, and assisted me in burying him on the peak of the bluff. I then returned to the village with my friends. I visited the grave of my old friend as I ascended Rock river the last time.

On my arrival at the village I was met by the chiefs and braves and conducted to the lodge which was prepared for me. After eating, I gave a fall account of all that I had seen and done. I explained to my people the manner in which the British and Americans fought. Instead of stealing upon each other and taking every advantage to kill the enemy and save their own people as we do, which, with us is considered good policy in a war chief, they march out in open daylight and fight regardless of the number of warriors they may lose. After the battle is over they retire to feast and drink wine as if nothing had happened. After which they make a statement in writing of what they have done, each party claiming the victory, and neither giving an account of half the number that have been killed on their own side They all fought like braves, but would not do to lead a party with us. Our maxim is: "Kill the enemy and save our own men." Those chiefs will do to paddle a canoe but not to steer it. The Americans shot better than the British, but their soldiers were not so well clothed, nor so well provided for.

The village chief informed me that after I started with my braves and the parties who followed, the nation was reduced to a small party of fighting men; that they would have been unable to defend themselves if the Americans had attacked them. That all the children and old men and women belonging to the warriors who had joined the British were left with them to provide for. A council had been called which agreed that Quashquame, the Lance, and other chiefs, with the old men, women and children, and such others as chose to accompany them, should descend the Mississippi to St. Louis, and place themselves under the American chief stationed there. They accordingly went down to St. Louis, were received as the friendly band of our nation, were sent up the Missouri and provided for, while their friends were assisting the British!

Keokuk was then introduced to me as the war chief of the braves then in the village. I inquired how he had become chief? They said that a large armed force was seen by their spies going toward Peoria. Fears were entertained that they would come up and attack the village and a council had been called to decide as to the best course to be adopted, which concluded upon leaving the village and going to the west side of the Mississippi to get out of the way. Keokuk, during the sitting of the council, had been standing at the door of the lodge, not being allowed to enter, as he had never killed an enemy, where he remained until old Wacome came out. He then told him that he heard what they had decided upon, and was anxious to be permitted to speak before the council adjourned. Wacome returned and asked leave for Keokuk to come in and make a speech. His request was granted. Keokuk entered and addressed the chiefs. He said: "I have heard with sorrow that you have determined to leave our village and cross the Mississippi, merely because you have been told that the Americans were coming in this direction. Would you leave our village, desert our homes and fly before an enemy approaches? Would you leave all, even the graves of our fathers, to the mercy of an enemy without trying to defend them? Give me charge of your warriors and I'll defend the village while you sleep in safety."

The council consented that Keokuk should be war chief. He marshalled his braves, sent out his spies and advanced with a party himself on the trail leading to Peoria. They returned without seeing an enemy. The Americans did not come by our village. All were satisfied with the appointment of Keokuk. He used every precaution that our people should not be surprised. This is the manner in which and the cause of his receiving the appointment.

I was satisfied, and then started to visit my wife and children. I found them well, and my boys were growing finely. It is not customary for us to say much about our women, as they generally perform their part cheerfully and never interfere with business belonging to the men. This is the only wife I ever had or ever will have. She is a good woman, and teaches my boys to be brave. Here I would have rested myself and enjoyed the comforts of my lodge, but I could not. I had promised to avenge the death of my adopted son.

I immediately collected a party of thirty braves, and explained to them the object of my making this war party, it being to avenge the death of my adopted son, who had been cruelly and wantonly murdered by the whites. I explained to them the pledge I had made to his father, and told them that they were the last words that he had heard spoken. All were willing to go with me to fulfill my word. We started in canoes, and descended the Mississippi, until we arrived ear the place where Fort Madison had stood. It had been abandoned and burned by the whites, and nothing remained but the chimneys. We were pleased to see that the white people had retired from the country. We proceeded down the river again. I landed with one brave near Cape Gray, the remainder of the party went to the mouth of the Quiver. I hurried across to the tail that led from the mouth of the Quiver to a fort, and soon after heard firing at the mouth of the creek. Myself and brave concealed ourselves on the side of the road. We had not remained here long before two men, riding one horse, came at full speed from the direction of the sound of the firing. When they came sufficiently near we fired; the horse jumped and both men fell. We rushed toward them and one rose and ran. I followed him and was gaining on him, when he ran over a pile of rails that had lately been made, seized a stick and struck at me. I now had an opportunity to see his face, and I knew him. He had been at Quashquame's village to teach his people how to plow. We looked upon him as a good man. I did not wish to kill him, and pursued him no further. I returned and met my brave. He said he had killed the other man and had his scalp in his hand. We had not proceeded far before we met the man supposed to be killed, coming up the road, staggering like a drunken man, and covered all over with blood. This was the most terrible sight I had ever seen. I told my comrade to kill him to put him out of his misery. I could not look at him. I passed on and heard a rustling in the bushes. I distinctly saw two little boys concealing themselves in the undergrowth, thought of my own children, and passed on without noticing them. My comrade here joined me, and in a little while we met the other detachment of our party. I told them that we would be pursued, and directed them to follow me. We crossed the creek and formed ourselves in the timber. We had not been here long, when a party of mounted men rushed at full speed upon us. I took deliberate aim and shot the leader of the party. He fell lifeless from his horse. All my people fired, but without effect. The enemy rushed upon us without giving us time to reload. They surrounded us and forced us into a deep sink-hole, at the bottom of which there were some bushes. We loaded our gum and awaited the approach of the enemy. They rushed to the edge of the hole, fired on us and killed one of our men. We instantly returned their fire, killing one of their party. We reloaded and commenced digging holes in the side of the bank to protect ourselves, while a party watched the enemy, expecting their whole force would be upon us immediately. Some of my warriors commenced singing their death songs. I heard the whites talking, and called to them to come out and fight. I did not like my situation and wished the matter settled. I soon heard chopping and knocking. I could not imagine what they were doing. Soon after they ran up a battery on wheels and fired without hurting any of us. I called to them again, and told them if they were brave men to come out and fight us. They gave up the siege and returned to their fort about dusk. There were eighteen in this trap with me. We came out unharmed, with the exception of the brave who was killed by the enemy's fist fire, after we were entrapped. We found one white man dead at the edge of the sink-hole, whom they did not remove for fear of our fire, and scalped him, placing our dead brave upon him, thinking we could not leave him in a better situation than on the prostrate form of a fallen foe.

We had now effected our purpose and concluded to go back by land, thinking it unsafe to use our canoes. I found my wife and children, and the greater part of our people, at the mouth of the Iowa river. I now determined to remain with my family and hunt for them, and to humble myself before the Great Spirit, returning thanks to him for preserving me through the war. I made my hunting camp on English river, which is a branch of the Iowa. During the winter a party of Pottawattomies came from the Illinois to pay me a visit, among them was Washeown, an old man who had formerly lived in our village. He informed as that in the fall the Americans had built a fort at Peoria and had prevented them from going down the Sangamon to hunt. He said they were very much distressed. Gomo had returned from the British army, and brought news of their defeat near Malden. He told us that he went to the American chief with a flag, gave up fighting, and told him he desired to make peace for his nation. The American chief gave him a paper to the war chief at Peoria, and I visited that fort with Gomo. It was then agreed that there should be no more hostilities between the Americans and the Pottawattomies. Two of the white chiefs, with eight Pottawattomie braves, and five others, Americans, had gone down to St. Louis to have the treaty of peace confirmed. This, said Washeown, is good news; for we can now go to our hunting grounds, and, for my part, I never had anything to do with this war. The Americans never killed any of our people before the war, nor interfered with our hunting grounds, and I resolved to do nothing against them. I made no reply to these remarks as the speaker was old and talked like a child.

We gave the Pottawattomies a great feast. I presented Washeown with a good horse. My braves gave one to each of his party, and, at parting, said they wished us to make peace, which we did not promise, but told them that we would not send out war parties against the settlements.

A short time after the Pottawattomies had gone, a party of thirty braves belonging to our nation, from the peace camp on the Missouri, paid us a visit. They exhibited five scalps which they had taken on the Missouri, and wished us to join in a dance over them, which we willingly did. They related the manner in which they had taken these scalps. Myself and braves showed them the two we had taken near the Quiver, and told them the cause that induced us to go out with the war party, as well as the manner in which we took these scalps, and the difficulty we had in obtaining them.

They recounted to us all that had taken place, the number that had been slain by the peace party, as they were called and recognized to be, which far surpassed what our warriors, who had joined the British, had done. This party came for the purpose of joining the British, but I advised them to return to the peace party, and told them the news which the Pottawattomies had brought. They returned to the Missouri, accompanied by some of my braves whose families were there.

After "sugar-making" was over in the spring, I visited the Fox village at the lead mines. They had nothing to do with the war, and consequently were not in mourning. I remained there some days, spending my time very pleasantly with them in dancing and feasting. I then paid a visit to the Pottawattomie village on the Illinois river, and learned that Sanatuwa and Tatapuckey had been to St. Louis. Gomo told me that "peace had been made between his people and the Americans, and that seven of his band remained with the war chief to make the peace stronger." He then told me: "Washeown is dead! He had gone to the fort to carry some wild fowl to exchange for tobacco, pipes and other articles. He had secured some tobacco and a little flour, and left the fort before sunset, but had not proceeded far when he was *shot dead* by a white war chief, who had concealed himself near the path for that purpose. He then dragged him to the lake and threw him in, where I afterwards found him. I have since given two homes and a rifle to his relatives, not to break the peace, to which they have agreed."

I remained for sometime at the village of Gomo, and went with him to the fort to pay a visit to the war chief. I spoke the Pottawattomie tongue well, and was taken for one of their people by him. He treated us friendly, and said he was very much displeased about the murder of Washeown. He promised us he would find out and punish the person who killed him. He made some inquiries about the Sacs, which I answered. On my return to Rock river, I was informed that a party of soldiers had gone up the Mississippi to build a fort at Prairie du Chien. They stopped near our village, appearing very friendly, and were treated kindly by our people.

We commenced repairing our lodges, putting our village in order, and clearing our cornfields. We divided the fields belonging to the party on the Missouri among those who wanted them, on condition that they should be relinquished to their owners on their return from the peace establishment. We were again happy in our village. Our women went cheerfully to work and all moved on harmoniously.

Sometime afterward, five or six boats arrived loaded with soldiers on their way to Prairie du Chien to reinforce the garrison at that place. They appeared friendly and were well received, and we held a council with the war chief. We had no intention of hurting him or any of his party, for we could easily have defeated them. They remained with us all day and gave oar people plenty of whisky. Doing the night a party arrived, by way of Rock river, who brought us six kegs of powder. They told us that the British had gone to Prairie du Chien and taken the fort. They wished us to again join them in the war, which we agreed to do. I collected my warriors and determined to pursue the boats, which had sailed with a fair wind. If we had known the day before, we could easily have taken them all, as the war chief used no precaution to prevent it.

I started immediately with my party, by land, in pursuit, thinking that some of their boats might get aground, or that the Great Spirit would put them in our power, if he wished them taken and their people killed. About half way up the rapids I had a full view of the boats all sailing with a strong wind. I discovered that one boat was badly managed, and was suffered to be drawn ashore by the wind. They landed by running hard aground and lowered their sail. The others passed on. This boat the Great Spirit gave to us. All that could, hurried aboard, but they were unable to push off, being fast aground. We advanced to the river's bank undercover, and commenced firing on the boat. I encouraged my braves to continue firing. Several guns were fired from the boat, but without effect. I prepared my bow and arrows to throw fire to the sail, which was lying on the boat. After two or three attempts, I succeeded in setting it on fire. The boat was soon in flames. About this time, one of the boats that had passed returned, dropped anchor and swung in close to one which was on fire, taking off all the people except those who were killed or badly wounded. We could distinctly see them passing from one boat to the other, and fired on them with good effect. We wounded the war chief in this way. Another boat now came down, dropped her anchor, which did not take hold, and drifted whore. The other boat cut her cable and drifted down the river, leaving their comrades without attempting to assist them. We then commenced an attack upon this boat, firing several rounds, which was not returned. We thought they were afraid or only had a few aboard. I therefore ordered a rush toward the boat, but when we got near enough they fired, killing two of our braves—these being all we lost in the engagement. Some of their men jumped out and shoved the boat off, and thus got away without losing a man. I had a good opinion of this war chief, as he managed so much better than the others. It would give me pleasure to shake him by the hand.

We now put out the fire on the captured boat to save the cargo, when a skiff was seen coming down the river. Some of our people cried out, "Here comes an express from Prairie du Chien." We hoisted the British flag, but they would not land. They turned their little boat around, and rowed up the river. We directed a few shots at them, but they were so far off that we could not hurt them. I found several barrels of whisky on the captured boat, knocked in the heads and emptied the bad medicine late the river. I next found a box full of small bottles and packages, which appeared to be bad medicine also, such as the medicine men kill the white people with when they are sick. This I threw into the river. Continuing my search for plunder, I found several guns, some large barrels filled with clothing, and a number of cloth lodges, all of which I distributed among my warriors. We now disposed of the dead, and returned to the Fox village opposite the lower end of Rock Island, where we put up our new lodges, and hoisted the British flag. A great many of our braves were dressed in the uniform clothing which we had taken from the Americans, which gave our encampment the appearance of a regular camp of soldiers. We placed out sentinels and commenced dancing over the scalps we had taken. Soon after several boats passed down, among them a very large one carrying big guns. Our young men followed them some distance, but could do them no damage more than scare them. We were now certain that the fort at Prairie du Chien had been taken, as this large boat went up with the first party who built the fort.

In the course of the day some of the British came down in a small boat. They had followed the large one, thinking it would get fast in the rapids, in which case they were sure of taking her. They had summoned her on her way down to surrender, but she refused to do so, and now, that she had passed the rapids in safety, all hope of taking her had vanished. The British landed a big gun and gave us three soldiers to manage it. They complimented us for our bravery in taking the boat, and told us what they had done at Prairie do Chien. They gave us, a keg of rum, and joined with us in our dancing and feasting. We gave them somethings which we had taken from the boat, particularly books and papers. They started the next morning, promising to return in a few days with a large body of soldiers.

We went to work under the direction of the men left with us, and dug up the ground in two places to put the big gun in, that the men might remain in with it and be safe. We then sent spies down the river to reconnoitre, who sent word by a runner that several boats were coming up filled with men. I marshalled my forces and was soon ready for their arrival. I resolved to fight, as we had not yet had a fair fight with the Americans during the war. The boats arrived in the evening, stopping at a small willow island, nearly opposite to us. During the night we removed our big gun further down, and at daylight next morning commenced firing. We were pleased to see that almost every shot took effect. The British being good gunners, rarely missed. They pushed off as quickly as possible, although I had expected they would land and give us battle. I was fully prepared to meet them but was sadly disappointed by the boats all sailing down the river. A party of braves followed to watch where they landed, but they did not stop until they got below the Des Moines rapids, where they came ashore and commenced building a fort. I did not want a fort in our country, as we wished to go down to the Two River country in the fall and hunt, it being our choice hunting ground, and we concluded that if this fort was built, it would prevent us from going there. We arrived in the vicinity in the evening, and encamped on a high bluff for the night. We made no fire, for fear of being observed, and our young men kept watch by turns while others slept. I was very tired, and was soon asleep. The Great Spirit, during my slumber, told me to go down the bluff to a creek, that I would there find a hollow tree cut down, and by looking in at the top of it, I would see a large snake with head erect—to observe the direction he was looking, and I would see the enemy close by and unarmed. In the morning I communicated to my braves what the Great Spirit had said to me, took one of them and went down a ravine that led to the creek. I soon came in sight of the place where they were building the fort, which was on a hill at the opposite side of the creek. I saw a great many men. We crawled cautiously on our hands and knees until we got to the bottom land, then through the grass and weeds until we reached the bank of the creek. Here I found a tree that had been cut down; I looked in at the top of it and saw a large snake, with his head raised, looking across the creek. I raised myself cautiously, and discovered nearly opposite to me, two war chiefs walking arm in arm, without guns. They turned and walked back toward the place where the men were working at the fort. In a little while they returned, walking directly towards the spot where we lay concealed, but did not come so near as before. If they had they would have been killed, for each of us had a good rifle. We crossed the creek and crawled to a cluster of bushes. I again raised myself a little to see if they were coming; but they went into the fort, and by this they saved their lives.

We recrossed the creek and I returned alone, going up the same ravine I came down. My brave went down the creek, and I, on raising the brow of a hill to the left of the one we came down, could plainly see the men at work. I saw a sentinel walking in the bottom near the mouth of the creek. I watched him attentively, to see if he perceived my companion, who had gone toward him. The sentinel stopped for sometime and looked toward where my brave was concealed. He walked first one way and then the other.

I observed my brave creeping towards him, at last he lay still for a while, not even moving the grass, and as the sentinel turned to walk away, my brave fired and he fell. I looked towards the fort, and saw the whites were in great confusion, running wildly in every direction, some down the steep bank toward a boat. My comrade joined me, we returned to the rest of the party and all hurried back to Rock river, where we arrived in safety at our village. I hung up my medicine bag, put away my rifle and spear, feeling as if I should want them no more, as I had no desire to raise other war parties against the whites unless they gave me provocation. Nothing happened worthy of note until spring, except that the fort below the rapids had been abandoned and burned by the Americans.

Soon after I returned from my wintering ground we received information that peace had been made between the British and Americans, and that we were required to make peace also, and were invited to go down to Portage des Sioux, for that purpose. Some advised that we should go down, others that we should not. Nomite, our principal civil chief, said he would go, as soon as the Foxes came down from the mines.

They came and we all started from Rock river, but we had not gone far before our chief was taken sick and we stopped with him at the village on Henderson river. The Foxes went on and we were to follow as soon as our chief got better, but he rapidly became worse and soon died. His brother now became the principal chief. He refused to go down, saying, that if he started, he would be taken sick and die as his brother had done. This seemed to be reasonable, so we concluded that none of us would go at this time. The Foxes returned. They said, "we have smoked the pipe of peace with our enemies, and expect that the Americans will send a war party against you if you do not go down." This I did not believe, as the Americans had always lost by their armies that were sent against us. La Gutrie and other British traders arrived at our village in the fall. La Gutrie told us that we must go down and make peace, as this was the wish of our English father. He said he wished us to go down to the Two River country to winter, where game was plenty, as there had been no hunting there for several years.

Having heard the principal war chief had come up with a number of troops, and commenced the erection of a fort near the Rapids des Moines, we consented to go down with the traders to visit the American chief, and tell him the reason why we had not been down sooner. When we arrived at the head of the rapids, the traders left their goods, and all of their boats with one exception, in which they accompanied us to see the Americans. We visited the war chief on board his boat, telling him what we had to say, and explaining why we had not been down sooner. He appeared angry and talked to La Gutrie for sometime. I inquired of him what the war chief said. He told me that he was threatening to hang him up to the yard arm of his boat. "But" said he, "I am not afraid of what he says. He dare not put his threats into execution. I have done no more than I had a right to do as a British subject."

I then addressed the chief, asking permission for ourselves and some Menomonees, to go down to the Two River country for the purpose of hunting. He said we might go down but must return before the ice came, as he did not intend that we should winter below the fort. "But," he inquired, "what do you want the Menomonee to go with you for?"

I did not know at first what reply to make, but told him that they had a great many pretty squaws with them, and we wished them to go with us on that account. He consented. We all went down the river and remained all winter, as we had no intention of returning before spring when we asked leave to go. We made a good hunt. Having loaded our trader's boats with furs and peltries, they started to Mackinac, and we returned to our village.

There is one circumstance that I did not relate at the proper place. It has no reference to myself or people, but to my friend Gomo, the Pottawattomie chief. He came to Rock river to pay me a visit, and during his stay he related to me the following story:

"The war chief at Peoria is a very good man. He always speaks the truth and treats our people well. He sent for me one day, told me he was nearly out of provisions, and wished me to send my young men hunting to supply his fort. I promised to do so, immediately returned to my camp and told my young men the wishes and wants of the war chief. They readily agreed to go and hurt for our friend and returned with plenty of deer. They carried them to the fort, laid them down at the gate and returned to our camp. A few days afterward I went again to the fort to see if they wanted anymore meat. The chief gave me powder and lead and said he wanted, me to send my hunters out again. When I returned to camp, I told my young men that the chief wanted more meat. Matatah, one of my principal braves, said he would take a party and go across the Illinois, about one day's travel, where game was plenty, and make a good hunt for our friend the war chief. He took eight hunters with him, and his wife and several other squaws went with them. They had travelled about half the day in the prairie when they discovered a party of white men coming towards them with a drove of cattle. Our hunters apprehended no danger or they would have kept out of the way of the whites, who had not yet perceived them. Matatah changed his course, as he wished to meet and speak to the whites. As soon as the whites saw our party, some of them put off at full speed, and came up to our hunters. Matatah gave up his gun to them, and endeavored to explain to them that he was friendly and was hunting for the war chief. They were not satisfied with this but fired at and wounded him. He got into the branches of a tree that had blown down, to keep the horses from running over him. He was again fired on several times and badly wounded. He, finding that he would be murdered, and, mortally wounded already, sprang at the man nearest him, seized his gun and shot him from his horse. He then fell, covered with blood from his wounds, and immediately expired. The other hunters being in the rear of Matatah attempted to escape, after seeing their leader so basely murdered by the whites. They were pursued and nearly all of the party killed. My youngest brother brought me the news in the night, he having been with the party and was slightly wounded. He said the whites had abandoned their cattle and gone back towards the settlement. The rest of the night we spent in mourning for our friends. At daylight I blacked my face and started for the fort to see the chief. I met him at the gate and told him what had happened. His countenance changed and I could see sorrow depicted in it for the death of my people. He tried to persuade me that I was mistaken, as he could not believe that the whites would act so cruelly. But when I convinced him, he said to me, 'those cowards who murdered your people shall be punished.' I told him that my people would have revenge, that they would not trouble any of his people at the fort, as we did not blame him or any of his soldiers, but that a party of my braves would go towards the Wabash to avenge the death of their friends and relations. The next day I took a party of hunters, killed several deer, and left them at the fort gate as I passed."

Here Gomo ended his story. I could relate many similar ones that have come within my own knowledge and observation, but I dislike to look back and bring on sorrow afresh. I will resume my narrative.

The great chief at St. Louis having sent word for us to come down and confirm the treaty, we did not hesitate, but started immediately that we might smoke the peace pipe with him. On our arrival we met the great chiefs in council. They explained to us the words of our Great Father at Washington, accusing us of heinous crimes and many misdemeanors, particularly in not coming down when first invited. We knew very well that our Great Father had deceived us and thereby forced us to join the British, and could not believe that he had put this speech into the mouths of those chiefs to deliver to us. I was not a civil chief and consequently made no reply, but our civil chiefs told the commissioner that, "What you say is a lie. Our Great Father sent us no such speech, he knew that the situation in which we had been placed was caused by him." The white chiefs appeared very angry at this reply and said, "We will break off the treaty and make war against you, as you have grossly insulted us."

Our chiefs had no intention of insulting them and told them so, saying, "we merely wish to explain that you have told us a lie, without any desire to make you angry, in the same manner that you whites do when you do not believe what is told you." The council then proceeded and the pipe of peace was smoked.

Here for the first time, I touched the goose quill to the treaty not knowing, however, that, by the act I consented to give away my village. Had that been explained to me I should have opposed it and never would have signed their treaty, as my recent conduct will clearly prove.

What do we know of the manners, the laws, and the customs of the white people? They might buy our bodies for dissection, and we would touch the goose quill to confirm it and not know what we were doing. This was the case with me and my people in touching the goose quill for the first time.

We can only judge of what is proper and right by our standard of what is right and wrong, which differs widely from the whites, if I have been correctly informed. The whites may do wrong all their lives, and then if they are sorry for it when about to die, all is well, but with us it is different. We must continue to do good throughout our lives. If we have corn and meat, and know of a family that have none, we divide with them. If we have more blankets than we absolutely need, and others have not enough, we must give to those who are in want. But I will presently explain our customs and the manner in which we live.

We were treated friendly by the whites and started on our return to our village on Rock river. When we arrived we found that the troops had come to build a fort on Rock Island. This, in our opinion, was a contradiction to what we had done—"to prepare for war in time of peace." We did not object, however, to their building their fort on the island, but were very sorry, as this was the best one on the Mississippi, and had long been the resort of our young people during the summer. It was our garden, like the white people have near their big villages, which supplied us with strawberries, blackberries, gooseberries, plums, apples and nuts of different kinds. Being situated at the foot of the rapids its waters supplied us with the finest fish. In my early life I spent many happy days on this island. A good spirit had charge of it, which lived in a cave in the rocks immediately under the place where the fort now stands. This guardian spirit has often been seen by our people. It was white, with large wings like a swan's, but ten times larger. We were particular not to make much noise in that part of the island which it inhabited, for fear of disturbing it. But the noise at the fort has since driven it away, and no doubt a bad spirit has taken its place.

Our village was situated on the north side of Rock river, at the foot of the rapids, on the point of land between Rock river and the Mississippi.

In front a prairie extended to the Mississippi, and in the rear a continued bluff gently ascended from the prairie.

Black Hawk's Tower

ON ITS HIGHEST PEAK OUR Watch Tower was situated, from which we had a fine view for many miles up and down Rock river, and in every direction. On the side of this bluff we had our corn fields, extending about two miles up parallel with the larger river, where they adjoined those of the Foxes, whose village was on the same stream, opposite the lower end of Rock Island, and three miles distant from ours. We had eight hundred acres in cultivation including what we had on the islands in Rock river. The land around our village which remained unbroken, was covered with blue-grass which furnished excellent pasture for our horses. Several fine springs poured out of the bluff near by, from which we were well supplied with good water. The rapids of Rock river furnished us with an abundance of excellent fish, and the land being very fertile, never failed to produce good crops of corn, beans, pumpkins and squashes. We always had plenty; our children never cried from hunger, neither were our people in want. Here our village had stood for more than a hundred years, during all of which time we were the undisputed possessors of the Mississippi valley, from the Wisconsin to the Portage des Sioux, near the mouth of the Missouri, being about seven hundred miles in length.

At this time we had very little intercourse with the whites except those who were traders. Our village was healthy, and there was no place in the country possessing such advantages, nor hunting grounds better than those we had in possession. If a prophet had come to our village in those days and told us that the things were to take place which have since come to pass, none of our people would have believed him. What! to be driven from our village, and our hunting grounds, and not even to be permitted to visit the graves of our forefathers and relatives and our friends?

This hardship is not known to the whites. With us it is a custom to visit the graves of our friends and keep them in repair for many years. The mother will go alone to weep over the grave of her child. The brave, with pleasure, visits the grave of his father, after he has been successful in war, and repaints the post that marks where he lies. There is no place like that where the bones of our forefathers lie to go to when in grief. Here prostrate by the tombs of our fathers will the Great Spirit take pity on us.

But how different is our situation now from what it was in those happy days. Then were we as happy as the buffalo on the plains, but now, we are as miserable as the hungry wolf on the prairie. But I am digressing from my story. Bitter reflections crowd upon my mind and must find utterance.

When we returned to our village in the spring, from our wintering grounds, we would finish bartering with our traders, who always followed us to our village. We purposely kept some of our fine furs for this trade, and, as there was great opposition among them, who should get these furs, we always got our goods cheap. After this trade was met, the traders would give us a few kegs of rum, which were generally promised in the fall, to encourage us to make a good hunt and not go to war. They would then start with their furs and peltries, for their homes, and our old men would take a frolic. At this time our young men never drank. When this was ended, the next thing to be done was to bury our dead; such as had died during the year. This is a great medicine feast. The relations of those who have died, give all the goods they have purchased, as presents to their friends, thereby reducing themselves to poverty, to show the Great Spirit that they are humble, so that he will take pity on them. We would next open the caches, take out the corn and other provisions which had been put up in the fall. We would then commence repairing our lodges. As soon as this was accomplished, we repair the fences around our corn fields and clean them off ready for planting. This work was done by the women. The men during this time are feasting on dried venison, bear's meat, wild fowl and corn prepared in different ways, while recounting to one another what took place during the winter.

Our women plant the corn, and as soon as they are done we make a feast, at which we dance the crane dance in which they join us, dressed in their most gaudy attire, and decorated with feathers. At this feast the young men select the women they wish to have for wives. He then informs his mother, who calls on the mother of the girl, when the necessary arrangements are made and the time appointed for him to come. He goes to the lodge when all are asleep, or pretend to be, and with his flint and steel strikes a light and soon finds where his intended sleeps. He then awakens her, holds the light close to his face that she may know him, after which he places the light close to her. If she blows it out the ceremony is ended and he appears in the lodge next morning as one of the family. If she does not blow out the light, but leaves it burning he retires from the lodge. The next day he places himself in full view of it and plays his flute. The young women go out one by one to see who he is playing for. The tune changes to let them know he is not playing for them. When his intended makes her appearance at the door, he continues his courting tune until she returns to the lodge. He then quits playing and makes another trial at night which mostly turns out favorable. During the first year they ascertain whether they can agree with each other and be happy, if not they separate and each looks for another companion. If we were to live together and disagree, we would be as foolish as the whites. No indiscretion can banish a woman from her parental lodge; no difference how many children she may bring home she is always welcome—the kettle is over the fire to feed them.

The crane dance often lasts two or three days. When this is over, we feast again and have our national dance. The large square in the village is swept and prepared for the purpose. The chiefs and old warriors take seats on mats, which have been spread on the upper end of the square, next come the drummers and singers, the braves and women form the sides, leaving a large space in the middle. The drums beat and the singing commences. A warrior enters the square keeping time with the music. He shows the manner he started on a war party, how he approached the enemy, he strikes and shows how he killed him. All join in the applause, and he then leaves the square and another takes his place. Such of our young men have not been out in war parties and killed in enemy stand back ashamed, not being allowed to enter the square. I remember that I was ashamed to look where our young men stood, before I could take my stand in the ring as a warrior.

What pleasure it is to an old warrior, to see his son come forward and relate his exploits. It makes him feel young, induces him to enter the square and "fight his battles o'er again."

This national dance makes our warriors. When I was travelling last summer on a steamboat on the river, going from New York to Albany, I was shown the place where the Americans dance the war-dance, (West Point), where the old warriors recount to their young men what they have done to stimulate them to go and do likewise. This surprised me, as I did not think the whites understood our way of making braves.

When our national dance is over, our cornfields hoed, every weed dug up and our corn about knee high, all our young men start in a direction toward sundown, to hunt deer and buffalo and to kill Sioux if any are found on our hunting grounds. A part of our old men and women go to the lead mines to make lead, and the remainder of our people start to fish and get meat stuff. Everyone leaves the village and remains away about forty days. They then return, the hunting party bringing in dried buffalo and deer meat, and sometimes Sioux scalps, when they are found trespassing on our hunting grounds. At other times they are met by a party of Sioux too strong for them and are driven in. If the Sioux have killed the Sacs last, they expect to be retaliated upon and will fly before them, and so with us. Each party knows that the other has a right to retaliate, which induces those who have killed last to give way before their enemy, as neither wishes to strike, except to avenge the death of relatives. All our wars are instigated by the relations of those killed, or by aggressions on our hunting grounds. The party from the lead mines brings lead, and the others dried fish, and mats for our lodges. Presents are now made by each party, the first giving to the others dried buffalo and deer, and they in return presenting them lead, dried fish and mats. This is a happy season of the year, having plenty of provisions, such as beans, squashes and other produce; with our dried meat and fish, we continue to make feasts and visit each other until our corn is ripe. Some lodge in the village a feast daily to the Great Spirit. I cannot explain this so that the white people will understand me, as we have no regular standard among us.

Everyone makes his feast as he thinks best, to please the Great Spirit, who has the care of all beings created. Others believe in two Spirits, one good and one bad, and make feasts for the Bad Spirit, to keep him quiet. They think that if they can make peace with him, the Good Spirit will not hurt them. For my part I am of the opinion, that so far as we have reason, we have a right to use it in determining what is right or wrong, and we should always pursue that path which we believe to be right, believing that "whatsoever is, is right." If the Great and Good Spirit wished us to believe and do as the whites, he could easily change our opinions, so that we could see, and think, and act as they do. We are nothing compared to his power, and we feel and know it. We have men among us, like the whites, who pretend to know the right path, but will not consent to show it without pay. I have no faith in their paths, but believe that every man must make his own path.

When our corn is getting ripe, our young people watch with anxiety for the signal to pull roasting ears, as none dare touch them until the proper time. When the corn is fit for use another great ceremony takes place, with feasting and returning thanks to the Great Spirit for giving us corn.

I will has relate the manner in which corn first came. According to tradition handed down to our people, a beautiful woman was seen to descend from the clouds, and alight upon the earth, by two of our ancestors who had killed a deer, and were sitting by a fire roasting a part of it to eat. They were astonished at seeing her, and concluded that she was hungry and had smelt the meat. They immediately went to her, taking with them a piece of the roasted venison. They presented it to her, she ate it, telling them to return to the spot where she was sitting at the end of one year, and they would find a reward for their kindness and generosity. She then ascended to the clouds and disappeared. The men returned to their village, and explained to the tribe what they had seen, done ad heard, but were laughed at by their people. When the period had arrived for them to visit this consecrated ground, where they were to find a reward for their attention to the beautiful woman of the clouds, they went with a large party, and found where her right hand had rested on the ground corn growing, where the left hand had rested beans, and immediately where she had been seated, tobacco.

The two first have ever since been cultivated by our people as our principal provisions, and the last is used for smoking. The white people have since found out the latter, and seem to it relish it as much as we do, as they use it in different ways: Smoking, snuffing and chewing.

We thank the Great Spirit for all the good he has conferred upon us. For myself, I never take a drink of water from a spring without being mindful of his goodness.

We next have our great ball play, from three to five hundred on a side play this game. We play for guns, lead, homes and blankets, or any other kind of property we may have. The successful party takes the stakes, and all return to our lodges with peace and friendship. We next commence horse racing, and continue on, sport and feasting until the corn is secured. We then prepare to leave our village for our hunting grounds.

The traders arrive and give us credit for guns, flints, powder, shot and lead, and such articles as we want to clothe our families with and enable us to hunt. We first, however, hold a council with them, to ascertain the price they will give for our skins, and then they will charge us for the goods. We inform them where we intend hunting, and tell them where to build their houses. At this place we deposit a part of our corn, and leave our old people. The traders have always been kind to them and relieved them when in want, and consequently were always much respected by our people, and never since we were a nation, has one of them been killed by our people.

We then disperse in small parties to make our hunt, and as soon as it is over, we return to our trader's establishment, with our skins, and remain feasting, playing cards and at other pastimes until the close of the winter. Our young men then start on the beaver hunt, others to hunt raccoons and muskrats; the remainder of our people go to the sugar camps to make sugar. All leave our encampment and appoint a place to meet on the Mississippi, so that we may return together to our village in the spring. We always spend our time pleasantly at the sugar camp. It being the season for wild fowl, we lived well and always had plenty, when the hunters came in that we might make a feast for them. After this is over we return to our village, accompanied sometimes by our traders. In this way the time rolled round happily. But these are times that were.

While on the subject of our manners and customs, it might be well to relate an instance that occurred near our village just five years before we left it for the last time.

In 1827, a young Sioux Indian got lost on the prairie, in a snow storm, and found his way into a camp of the Sacs. According to Indian customs, although he was an enemy, he was safe while accepting their hospitality. He remained there for sometime on account of the severity of the storm. Becoming well acquainted he fell in love with the daughter of the Sac at whose village he had been entertained, and before leaving for his own country, promised to come to the Sac village for her at a certain time during the approaching summer. In July he made his way to the Rock river village, secreting himself in the woods until he met the object of his love, who came out to the field with her mother to assist her in hoeing corn. Late in the afternoon her mother left her and went to the village. No sooner had she got out of hearing, than he gave a loud whistle which assured the maiden that he had returned. She continued hoeing leisurely to the end of the row, when her lover came to meet her, and she promised to come to him as soon as she could go to the lodge and get her blanket, and together they would flee to his country. But unfortunately for the lovers the girl's two brothers had seen the meeting, and after procuring their guns started in pursuit of them. A heavy thunderstorm was coming on at the time. The lovers hastened to, and took shelter under a cliff of rocks, at Black Hawk's watchtower. Soon after a loud peal of thunder was heard, the cliff of rocks was shattered in a thousand pieces, and the lovers buried beneath, while in full view of her pursuing brothers. This, their unexpected tomb, still remains undisturbed.

This tower to which my name had been applied, was a favorite resort and was frequently visited by me alone, when I could sit and smoke my pipe, and look with wonder and pleasure, at the grand scenes that were presented by the sun's rays, even across the mighty water. On one occasion a Frenchman, who had been making his home in our village, brought his violin with him to the tower, to play and dance for the amusement of a number of our people, who had assembled there, and while dancing with his back to the cliff accidentally fell over it and was killed by the fall. The Indians say that always at the same time of the year, soft strains of the violin can be heard near that spot.

On returning in the spring from oar hunting grounds, I had the pleasure of meeting our old friend, the trader of Peoria, at Rock Island. He came up in a boat from St. Louis, not as a trader, but as our Agent. We were well pleased to see him. He told us that he narrowly escaped falling into the hands of Dixon. He remained with us a short time, gave us good advice, and then returned to St. Louis.

The Sioux having committed depredations on our people, we sent out war parties that summer, who succeeded in killing fourteen.

I paid several visits to Fort Armstrong, at Rock Island, during the summer, and was always well received by the gentlemanly officers stationed there, who were distinguished for their bravery, and they never trampled upon an enemy's rights. Colonel George Davenport resided near the garrison, and being in connection with the American Fur Company, furnished us the greater portion of our goods. We were not as happy then, in our village, as formerly. Our people got more liquor from the small traders than customary. I used all my influence to prevent drunkenness, but without effect. As the settlements progressed towards us, we became worse off and more unhappy.

Many of our people, instead of going to the old hunting grounds, when game was plenty, would go near the settlements to hunt, and, instead of saving their skins, to pay the trader for goods furnished them in the fall, would sell them to the settlement for whisky, and return in the spring with their families almost naked, and without the means of getting anything for them.

About this time my eldest son was taken sick and died. He had always been a dutiful child and had just grown to manhood. Soon after, my youngest daughter, an interesting and affectionate child, died also. This was a hard stroke, because I loved my children. In my distress I left the noise of the village and built my lodge on a mound in the corn-field, and enclosed it with a fence, around which I planted corn and beans. Here I was with my family alone. I gave everything I had away, and reduced myself to poverty. The only covering I retained was a piece of buffalo robe. I blacked my face and resolved on fasting for twenty-four moons, for the loss of my two children—drinking only of water during the day, and eating sparingly of boiled corn at sunset. I fulfilled my promise, hoping that the Great Spirit would take pity on me.

My nation had now some difficulty with the Iowas. Our young men had repeatedly killed some of them, and the breaches had always been made up by giving presents to the relations of those killed. But the last council we had with them, we promised that in case anymore of their people were killed ours, instead of presents, we would give up the person or persons, who had done the injury. We made this determination known to our people, but notwithstanding this, one of our young men killed an Iowa the following winter.

A party of our people were about starting for the Iowa village to give the young man up, and I agreed to accompany them. When we were ready to start, I called at the lodge for the young man to go with us. He was sick, but willing to go, but his brother, however, prevented him and insisted on going to die in his place, as he was unable to travel. We started, and on the seventh day arrived in sight of the Iowa village, and within a short distance of it we halted ad dismounted. We all bid farewell to our young brave, who entered the village singing his death song, and sat down on the square in the middle of the village. One of the Iowa chiefs came out to us. We told him that we had fulfilled our promise, that we had brought the brother of the young man who had killed one of his people—that he had volunteered to come in his place, in consequence of his brother being unable to travel from sickness. We had no further conversation but mounted our horses and rode off. As we started I cast my eye toward the village, and observed the Iowas coming out of their lodges with spears and war clubs. We took the backward trail and travelled until dark—then encamped and made a fire. We had not been there long before we heard the sound of homes coming toward us. We seized our arms, but instead of an enemy it was our young brave with two horses. He told me that after we had left him, they menaced him with death for sometime—then gave him something to eat—smoked the pipe with him and made him a present of the two horses and some goods, and started him after us. When we arrived at on, village our people were much pleased, and for their noble and generous conduct on this occasion, not one of the Iowa people has been killed since by our nation.

That fall I visited Malden with several of my band, and was well treated by the agent of our British Father, who gave us a variety of presents. He also gave me a medal, and told me there never would be war between England and America again; but for my fidelity to the British, during the war that had terminated sometime before, requested me to come with my band and get presents every year, as Colonel Dixon had promised me.

I returned and hunted that winter on the Two Rivers. The whites were now settling the country fast. I was out one day hunting in a bottom, and met three white men. They accused me of killing their hogs. I denied it, but they would not listen to me. One of them took my gun out of my hand and fired it off—then took out the flint, gave it back to me and commenced beating me with sticks, ordering me at the same time to be off. I was so much bruised that I could not sleep for several nights.

Sometime after this occurrence, one of my camp cut a bee tree and carried the honey to his lodge. A party of white men soon followed him, and told him the bee tree was theirs, and that he had no right to cut it. He pointed to the honey and told them to take it. They were not satisfied with this, but took all the packs of skins that he had collected during the winter, to pay his trader and clothe his family with in the spring, and carried them off.

How could we like a people who treated us so unjustly? We determined to break up our camp for fear they would do worse, and when we joined our people in the spring a great many of them complained of similar treatment.

This summer our agent came to live at Rock Island. He treated us well and gave us good advice. I visited him and the trader very often during the summer, and for the first time heard talk of our having to leave our village. The trader, Colonel George Davenport, who spoke our language, explained to me the terms of the treaty that had been made, and said we would be obliged to leave the Illinois side of the Mississippi, and advised us to select a good place for our village and remove to it in the spring. He pointed out the difficulties we would have to encounter if we remained at our village on Rock river. He had great influence with the principal Fox chief, his adopted brother, Keokuk. He persuaded him to leave his village, go to the west side of the Mississippi and build another, which he did the spring following. Nothing was talked of but leaving our village. Keokuk had been persuaded to consent to go, and was using all his influence, backed by the war chief at Fort Armstrong and our agent and trader at Rock Island, to induce others to go with him. He sent the crier through our village, to inform our people that it was the wish of our Great Father that we should remove to the west side of the Mississippi, and recommended the Iowa river as a good place for the new village. He wished his party to make such arrangements, before they started on their winter's hunt, an to preclude the necessity of their returning to the village in the spring.

The party opposed to removing called on me for my opinion. I gave it freely, and after questioning Quashquame about the sale of our lands, he assured me that he "never had consented to the sale of our village." I now promised this party to be the leader, and raised the standard of opposition to Keokuk, with a full determination not to leave our village. I had an interview with Keokuk, to see if this difficulty could not be settled with our Great Father, and told him to propose to give any other land that our Great Father might choose, even our lead mines, to be peaceably permitted to keep the small point of land on which our village was situated. I was of the opinion that the white people had plenty of land and would never take our village from us. Keokuk promised to make an exchange if possible, and applied to our agent, and the great chief at St. Louis, who had charge of all the agents, for permission to go to Washington for that purpose.

This satisfied us for a time. We started to our hunting grounds with good hopes that something would be done for us. Doing the winter I received information that three families of whites had come to our village and destroyed some of our lodges, were making fences and dividing our cornfields for their own use. They were quarreling among themselves about their lines of division. I started immediately for Rock river, a distance of ten days' travel, and on my arrival found the report true. I went to my lodge and saw a family occupying it. I wished to talk to them but they could not understand me. I then went to Rock Island; the agent being absent, I told the interpreter what I wanted to say to these people, viz: "Not to settle on our lands, nor trouble our fences, that there was plenty of land in the country for them to settle upon, and that they must leave our village, as we were coming back to it in the spring." The interpreter wrote me a paper, I went back to the village and showed it to the intruders, but could not understand their reply. I presumed, however, that they would remove as I expected them to. I returned to Rock Island, passed the night there and had a long conversation with the trader. He advised me to give up and make my village with Keokuk on the Iowa river. I told him that I would not. The next morning I crossed the Mississippi on very bad ice, but the Great Spirit had made it strong, that I might pass over safe. I traveled three days farther to see the Winnebago sub-agent and converse with him about our difficulties. He gave no better news than the trader had done. I then started by way of Rock river, to see the Prophet, believing that he as a man of great knowledge. When we met, I explained to him everything as it was. He at once agreed that I was right, and advised me never to give up our village, for the whites to plow up the bones of our people. He said, that if we remained at our village, the whites would not trouble us, and advised me to get Keokuk, and the party that consented to go with him to the Iowa in the spring, to return and remain at our village.

I returned to my hunting ground, after an absence of one moon, and related what I had done. In a short time we came up to our village, and found that the whites had not left it, but that others had come, and that the greater part of our cornfields had been enclosed. When we landed the whites appeared displeased because we came back. We repaired the lodges that hid been left standing and built others. Keokuk came to the village, but his object was to persuade others to follow him to the Iowa. He had accomplished nothing towards making arrangements for us to remain, or to exchange other lands for our village. There was no more friendship existing between us. I looked upon him as a coward and no brave, to abandon his village to be occupied by strangers. What right had these people to our village, and our fields, which the Great Spirit had given us to live upon?

My reason teaches me that land cannot be sold. The Great Spirit gave it to his children to live upon and cultivate as far as necessary for their subsistence, and so long as they occupy and cultivate it they have the right to the soil, but if they voluntarily leave it, then any other people have a right to settle on it. Nothing can be sold but such things as can be carried away.

In consequence of the improvements of the intruders on our fields, we found considerable difficulty to get ground to plant a little corn. Some of the whites permitted us to plant small patches in the fields they had fenced, keeping all the best ground for themselves. Our women had great difficulty in climbing their fences, being unaccustomed to the kind, and were ill treated if they left a rail down.

One of my old friends thought he was safe. His cornfield was on a small island in Rock river. He planted his corn, it came up well, but the white man saw it; he wanted it, and took his teams over, ploughed up the crop and replanted it for himself. The old man shed tears, not for himself but on account of the distress his family would be in if they raised no corn. The white people brought whisky to our village, made our people drink, and cheated them out of their homes, guns and traps. This fraudulent system was carried to such an extent that I apprehended serious difficulties might occur, unless a stop was put to it. Consequently I visited all the whites and begged them not to sell my people whisky. One of them continued the practice openly; I took a party of my young men, went to his house, took out his barrel, broke in the head and poured out the whisky. I did this for fear some of 'the whites might get killed by my people when they were drunk.

Our people were treated very badly by the whites on many occasions. At one time a white man beat one of our women cruelly, for pulling a few suckers of corn out of his field to suck when she was hungry. At another time one of our young men was beat with clubs by two white men, for opening a fence which crossed our road to take his horse through. His shoulder blade was broken and his body badly braised, from the effects of which he soon after died.

Bad and cruel as our people were treated by the whites, not one of them was hurt or molested by our band. I hope this will prove that we are a peaceable people—having permitted ten men to take possession of our corn fields, prevent us from planting corn, burn our lodges, ill-treat our women, and beat to death our men without offering resistance to their barbarous cruelties. This is a lesson worthy for the white man to learn: to use forbearance when injured.

We acquainted our agent daily with our situation, and through him the great chief at St. Louis, and hoped that something would be done for us. The whites were complaining at the same time that we were intruding upon their rights. They made it appear that they were the injured party, and we the intruders. They called loudly to the great war chief to protect their property.

How smooth must be the language of the whites, when they can make right look like wrong, and wrong like right.

During this summer I happened at Rock Island, when a great chief arrived, whom I had known as the great chief of Illinois, (Governor Cole) in company with another chief who I have been told is a great writer (judge James Hall.) I called upon them and begged to explain the grievances to them, under which my people and I were laboring, hoping that they could do something for us. The great chief however, did not seem disposed to council with, me. He said he was no longer the chief of Illinois; that his children had selected another father in his stead, and that he now only ranked as they did. I was surprised at this talk, as I had always heard that he was a good brave and great chief. But the white people appear to never be satisfied. When they get a good father, they hold councils at the suggestion of some bad, ambitious man, who wants the place himself, and conclude among themselves that this man, or someother equally ambitious, would make a better father than they have, and nine times out of ten they don't get as good a one again.

I insisted on explaining to these chiefs the true situation of my people. They gave their assent. I rose and made a speech, in which I explained to them the treaty made by Quashquame, and three of our braves, according to the manner the trader and others had explained it to me. I then told them that Quashquame and his party positively denied having ever sold my village, and that as I had never known them to lie, I was determined to keep it in possession.

I told them that the white people had already entered our village, burned our lodges, destroyed on, fences, ploughed up our corn and beat our people. They had brought whisky into our country, made our people drunk, and taken from them their homes, guns and traps, and that I had borne all this injury, without suffering any of my braves to raise a hand against the whites.

My object in holding this council was to get the opinion of these two chiefs as to the best course for me to pursue. I had appealed in vain, time after time to our agent, who regularly represented our situation to the chief at St. Louis, whose duty it was to call upon the Great Father to have justice done to us, but instead of this we are told that the white people wanted our county and we must leave it for them!

I did not think it possible that our Great Father wished us to leave our village where we had lived so long, and where the bones of so many of our people had been laid. The great chief said that as he no longer had any authority he could do nothing for us, and felt sorry that it was not in his power to aid us, nor did he know how to advise us. Neither of them could do anything for us, but both evidently were very sorry. It would give e great pleasure at all times to take these two chiefs by the hand.

That fall I paid a visit to the agent before we started to our hunting grounds, to hear if he had any good news for me. He had news. He said that the land on which our village now stood was ordered to be sold to individuals, and that when sold our right to remain by treaty would be at an end, and that if we returned next spring we would be forced to remove.

We learned during the winter, that part of the land where our village stood had been sold to individuals, and that the trader at Rock Island, Colonel Davenport, had bought the greater part that had been sold. The reason was now plain to me why he urged us to remove. His object, we thought, was to get our lands. We held several councils that winter to determine what we should do. We resolved in one of them, to return to our village as usual in the spring. We concluded that if we were removed by force, that the trader, agent and others must be the cause, and that if they were found guilty of having driven us from our village they should be killed. The trader stood foremost on this list. He had purchased the land on which my lodge stood, and that of our graveyard also. We therefore proposed to kill him and the agent, the interpreter, the great chief at St. Louis, the war chiefs at Forts Armstrong, Rock Island and Keokuk, these being the principal persons to blame for endeavoring to remove us. Our women received bad accounts from the women who had been raising corn at the new village, of the difficulty of breaking the new prairie with hoes, and the small quantity of corn raised. We were nearly in the same condition with regard to the latter, it being the first time I ever knew our people to be in want of provisions.

I prevailed upon some of Keokuk's band to return this spring to the Rock river village, but Keokuk himself would not come. I hoped that he would get permission to go to Washington to settle our affairs with our Great Father. I visited the agent at Rock Island. He was displeased because we had returned to our village, and told me that we must remove to the west of the Mississippi. I told him plainly that we would not. I visited the interpreter at his house, who advised me to do as the agent had directed me. I then went to see the trader and upbraided him for buying our lands. He said that if he had not purchased them some person else would, and that if our Great Father would make an exchange with us, he would willingly give up the land he had purchased to the government. This I thought was fair, and began to think that he had not acted so badly as I had suspected. We again repaired our lodges and built others, as most of our village had been burnt and destroyed. Our women selected small patches to plant corn, where the whites had not taken them in their fences, and worked hard to raise something for our children to subsist upon.

I was told that according to the treaty, we had no right to remain on the lands sold, and that the government would force us to leave them. There was but a small portion however that had been sold, the balance remaining in the hands of the government. We claimed the right, if we had no other, to "live and hunt upon it as long as it remained the property of the government," by a stipulation in the treaty that required us to evacuate it after it had been sold. This was the land that we wished to inhabit and thought we had a right to occupy.

I heard that there was a great chief on the Wabash, and sent a party to get his advice. They informed him that we had not sold our village. He assured them then, that if we had not sold the land on which our village stood, our Great Father would not take it from us.

I started early to Malden to see the chief of my British Father, and told him my story. He gave the same reply that the chief on the Wabash had given, and in justice to him I must say he never gave me any bad advice, but advised me to apply to our American Father, who, he said, would do us justice. I next called on the great chief at Detroit and made the same statement to him that I had made to the chief of our British Father. He gave me the same reply. He said if we had not sold our lands, and would remain peaceably on them, that we would not be disturbed. This assured me that I was right, and determined me to hold out as I had promised my people. I returned from Malden late in the fall. My people were gone to their hunting ground, whither I followed. Here I learned that they had been badly treated all summer by the whites, and that a treaty had been held at Prairie du Chien. Keokuk and some of our people attended it, and found that our Great Father had exchanged a small strip of the land that had been ceded by Quashquame and his party, with the Pottowattomies for a portion of their lead near Chicago. That the object of this treaty was to get it back again, and that the United States had agreed to give them sixteen thousand dollars a year, forever for this small strip of land, it being less than a twentieth part of that taken from our nation for one thousand dollars a year. This bears evidence of something I cannot explain. This land they say belonged to the United States. What reason then, could have induced them to exchange it with the Pottowattomies if it was so valuable? Why not keep it? Or if they found they had made a bad bargain with the Pottowattomies, why not take back their land at a fair proportion of what they gave our nation for it! If this small portion of the land that they took from us for one thousand dollars a year, be worth sixteen thousand dollars a year forever to the Pottowattomies, then the whole tract of country taken from us ought to be worth, to our nation, twenty times as much a this small fraction.

Here I was again puzzled to find out how the white people reasoned, and began to doubt whether they had any standard of right and wrong.

Communication was kept up between myself and the Prophet. Runners were sent to the Arkansas, Red river and Texas, not on the subject of our lands, but on a secret mission, which I am not at present permitted to explain.

It was related to me that the chiefs and head men of the Foxes had been invited to Prairie du Chien, to hold a Council for the purpose of settling the difficulties existing between them and the Sioux.

The chiefs and head men, amounting to nine, started for the place designated, taking with them one woman, and were met by the Menonomees and Sioux, near the Wisconsin and killed, all except one man. Having understood that the whole matter was published shortly after it occurred, and is known to the white people, I will say no more about it.

I would here remark, that our pastimes and sports had been laid aside for two years. We were a divided people, forming two parties. Keokuk being at the head of one, willing to barter our rights merely for the good opinion of the whites, and cowardly enough to desert our village to them. I was at the head of the other division, and was determined to hold on to my village, although I had been ordered to leave it. But, I considered, as myself and band had no agency in selling our county, and that, as provision had been made in the treaty, for us all to remain on it as long as it belonged to the United States, that we could not be forced away. I refused therefore to quit my village. It was here that I was born, and here lie the bones of many friends and relations. For this spot I felt a sacred reverence, and never could consent to leave it without being forced therefrom.

When I called to mind the scenes of my youth and those of later days, when I reflected that the theatre on which these were acted, had been so long the home of my fathers, who now slept on the hills around it, I could not bring my mind to consent to leave this country to the whites for any earthly consideration.

The winter passed off in gloom. We made a bad hunt for want of guns, traps and other necessaries which the whites had taken from our people for whisky. The prospect before me was a bad one. I fasted and called upon the Great Spirit to direct my steps to the right path. I was in great sorrow because all the whites with whom I was acquainted and had been on terms of intimacy, advised me contrary to my wishes, that I began to doubt whether I had a friend among them.

Keokuk, who has a smooth tongue, and is a great speaker, was busy in persuading my band that I was wrong, and thereby making many of them dissatisfied with me. I had one consolation, for all the women were on my side on account of their cornfields.

On my arrival again at my village, with my band increased, I found it worse than before. I visited Rock Island and the agent again ordered me to quit my village. He said that if we did not, troops would be sent to drive us off. He reasoned with me and told me it would be better for us to be with the rest of our people, so that we might avoid difficulty and live in peace. The interpreter joined him and gave me so many good reasons that I almost wished I had not undertaken the difficult task I had pledged myself to my brave band to perform. In this mood I called upon the trader, who is fond of talking, and had long been my friend, but now amongst those who advised me to give up my village. He received me very friendly and went on to defend Keokuk in what he had done, endeavoring to show me that I was bringing distress on our women and children. He inquired if some terms could not be made that would be honorable to me and satisfactory to my braves, for us to remove to the west side of the Mississippi. I replied that if our Great Father could do us justice and make the proposition, I could then give up honorably. He asked me "if the great chief at St. Louis would give us six thousand dollars to purchase provisions and other articles, if I would give up peaceably and remove to the west side of the Mississippi?" After thinking sometime I agreed that I could honorably give up, being paid for it, according to our customs, but told him that I could not make the proposal myself, even if I wished, because it would be dishonorable in me to do so. He said that he would do it by sending word to the great chief at St. Louis that he could remove us peaceably for the amount stated, to the west side of the Mississippi. A steamboat arrived at the island during my stay. After its departure the trader told me that he had requested a war chief, who was stationed at Galena, and was on board the steamboat, to make the offer to the great chief at St. Louis, and that he would soon be back and bring his answer. I did not let my people know what had taken place for fear they would be displeased. I did not much like what had been done myself, and tried to banish it from my mind.

After a few days had passed the war chief returned and brought an answer that "the great chief at St. Louis would give us nothing, and that if we did not remove immediately we would be driven off."

I was not much displeased with the answer they brought me, because I would rather have laid my bones with those of my forefathers than remove for any consideration. Yet if a friendly offer had been made as I expected, I would, for the sake of our women and children have removed peaceably.

I now resolved to remain in my village, and make no resistance if the military came, but submit to my fate. I impressed the importance of this course on all my band, and directed them in case the military came not to raise an arm against them.

About this time our agent was put out of office, for what reason I could never ascertain. I then thought it was for wanting to make us leave our village and if so it was right, because I was tired of hearing him talk about it. The interpreter, who had been equally as bad in trying to persuade us to leave our village was retained in office, and the young man who took the place of our agent, told the same old story over about removing us. I was then satisfied that this could not have been the cause.

Our women had planted a few patches of corn which was growing finely, and promised a subsistence for our children, but the white people again commenced ploughing it up. I now determined to put a stop to it by clearing our county of the intruders. I went to their principal men and told them that they should and must leave our country, giving them until the middle of the next day to remove. The worst left within the time appointed, but the one who remained, represented that his family, which was large, would be in a starving condition, if he went and left his crop. He promised to behave well, if I would consent to let him remain until fall, in order to secure his crop. He spoke reasonably and I consented.

We now resumed some of our games and pastimes, having been assured by the prophet that we would not be removed. But in a little while it was ascertained that a great war chief, General Gaines, was on his way to Rock river with a great number of soldiers. I again called upon the prophet, who requested a little time to see into the matter. Early next morning he came to me and said he had been dreaming;

that he saw nothing bad in this great war chief, General Gaines, who was now near Rock river. That his object was merely to frighten us from our village, that the white people might get our land for nothing. He assured us that this great war chief dare not, and would not, hurt any of us. That the Americans were at peace with the British, and when they made peace, the British required, and the Americans agreed to it, that they should never interrupt any nation of Indians that was at peace, and that all we had to do to retain our village was to refuse any and every offer that might be made by this war chief.

The war chief arrived and convened a council at the agency. Keokuk and Wapello were sent for, and with a number of their band were present.

The council house was opened and all were admitted, and myself and band were sent for to attend. When we arrived at the door singing a war song, and armed with lances, spears, war clubs, bows and arrows, as if going to battle, I halted and refused to enter, as I could see no necessity or propriety in having the room crowded with those who were already there. If the council was convened for us, why then have others in our room. The war chief having sent all out except Keokuk, Wapello and a few of their chiefs and braves, we entered the council in this warlike appearance, being desirous of showing the war chief that we were not afraid. He then rose and made a speech. He said:

"The president is very sorry to be put to the trouble and expense of sending so large a body of soldiers here to remove you from the lands you have long since ceded to the United States. Your Great Father has already warned you repeatedly, through your agent, to leave the country, and he is very sorry to find that you have disobeyed his orders. Your Great Father wishes you well, and asks nothing from you but what is reasonable and right. I hope you will consult your own interests, and leave the country you are occupying, and go to the other side of the Mississippi."

I replied:

"We have never sold our country. We never received any annuities from our American father, and we are determined to hold on to our village."

The war chief, apparently angry, rose and said

"Who is *Black Hawk*? Who is *Black Hawk*?"

I replied:

"I am a *Sac*! My forefather was a SAC! I and all the nations call me a SAC!!"

The war chief said:

"I came here neither to beg nor hire you to leave your village. My business is to remove you, peaceably if I can, forcibly if I must! I will now give you two days in which to remove, and if you do not cross the Mississippi by that time, I will adopt measures to force you away."

I told him that I never would consent to leave my village and was determined not to leave it.

The council broke up and the war chief retired to his fort. I consulted the prophet again. He said he had been dreaming, and that the Great Spirit had directed that a woman, the daughter of Mattatas, the old chief of the village, should take a stick in her hand and go before the war chief, and tell him that she is the daughter of Mattatas, and that he had always been the white man's friend. That he had fought their battles, been wounded in their service and had always spoken well of them, and she had never heard him say that he had sold their village. The whites are numerous, and can take it from us if they choose, but she hoped they would not be so unfriendly. If they were, he had one favor to ask; she wished her people to be allowed to remain long enough to gather their provisions now growing in their fields; that she was a woman and had worked hard to raise something to support her children. And now, if we are driven from our village without being allowed to save our corn, many of our little children must perish with hunger.

Accordingly Mattatas' daughter was sent to the fort, accompanied by several of our young men and was admitted. She went before the war chief and told the story of the prophet. The war chief said that the president did not send him here to make treaties with the women, nor to hold council with them. That our young men most leave the fort, but she might remain if she wished.

All our plans were defeated. We must cross the river, or return to our village and await the coming of the war chief with his soldiers. We determined on the latter, but finding that our agent, interpreter, trader and Keokuk, were determined on breaking my ranks, and had induced several of my warriors to cross the Mississippi, I sent a deputation to the agent, at the request of my band, pledging myself to leave the county in the fall, provided permission was given us to remain, and secure our crop of corn then growing, as we would be in a starving situation if we were driven off without the means of subsistence.

The deputation returned with an answer from the war chief, "That no further time would be given than that specified, and if we were not then gone he would remove us."

I directed my village crier to proclaim that my orders were, in the event of the war chief coming to our village to remove us, that not a gun should be fired or any resistance offered. That if he determined to fight, for them to remain quietly in their lodges, and let him kill them if he chose.

I felt conscious that this great war chief would not hurt our people, and my object was not war. Had it been, we would have attacked and killed the war chief and his braves, when in council with us, as they were then completely in our power. But his manly conduct and soldierly deportment, his mild yet energetic manner, which proved his bravery, forbade it.

Some of our young men who had been out as spies came in and reported that they had discovered a large body of mounted men coming toward our village, who looked like a war party. They arrived and took a position below Rock river, for their place of encampment. The great war chief, General Gaines, entered Rock river in a steamboat, with his soldiers and one big gun. They passed and returned close by our village, but excited no alarm among my braves. No attention was paid to the boat; even our little children who were playing on the bank of the river, as usual, continued their amusement. The water being shallow, the boat got aground, which gave the whites some trouble. If they had asked for assistance, there was not a brave in my band who would not willingly have aided them. Their people were permitted to pass and repass through our village, and were treated with friendship by our people.

The war chief appointed the next day to remove us. I would have remained and been taken prisoner by the regulars, but was afraid of the multitude of pale faced militia, who were on horse back, as they were under no restraint of their chiefs.

We crossed the river during the night, and encamped some distance below Rock Island. The great war chief convened another council, for the purpose of making a treaty with us. In this treaty he agreed to give us corn in place of that we had left growing in our fields. I touched the goose quill to this treaty, and was determined to live in peace.

The corn that had been given us was soon found to be inadequate to our wants, when loud lamentations were heard in the camp by the women and children, for their roasting ears, beans and squashes. To satisfy them, a small party of braves went over in the night to take corn from their own fields. They were discovered by the whites and fired upon. Complaints were again made of the depredations committed by some of my people, on their own corn fields.

I understood from our agent, that there had been a provision made in one of our treaties for assistance in agriculture, and that we could have our fields plowed if we required it. I therefore called upon him, and requested him to have a small log home built for me, and a field plowed that fall, as I wished to live retired. He promised to have it done. I then went to the trader, Colonel Davenport, and asked for permission to be buried in the graveyard at our village, among my old friends and warriors, which he gave cheerfully. I then returned to my people satisfied.

A short time after this, a party of Foxes went up to Prairie du Chien to avenge the murder of their chiefs and relations, which had been committed the summer previous, by the Menomonees and Sioux. When they arrived in the vicinity of the encampment of the Menomonees, they met with a Winnebago, and inquired for the Menomonee camp. They requested him to go on before them and see if there were any Winnebagoes in it, and if so, to tell them that they had better return to their own camp. He went and gave the information, not only to the Winnebagoes, but to the Menomonees, that they might be prepared. The party soon followed, killed twenty-eight Menomonees, and made their escape.

This retaliation which with us is considered lawful and right, created considerable excitement among the whites. A demand was made for the Foxes to be surrendered to, and tried by, the white people. The principal men came to me during the fall and asked my advice. I conceived that they had done right, and that our Great Father acted very unjustly in demanding them, when he had suffered all their chiefs to be decoyed away, and murdered by the Menomonees, without ever having made a similar demand of them. If he had no right in the first instance he had none now, and for my part, I conceived the right very questionable, if not an act of usurpation in any case, where a difference exists between two nations, for him to interfere. The Foxes joined my band with the intention to go out with them on the fall hunt.

About this time, Neapope, who started to Malden when it was ascertained that the great war chief, General Gaines, was coming to remove us, returned. He said he had seen the chief of our British Father, and asked him if the Americans could force us to leave our village. He said: "If you had not sold your land the Americans could not take your village from you. That the right being vested in you only, could be transferred by the voice and will of the whole nation, and that as you have never given your consent to the sale of your country, it yet remains your exclusive property, from which the American government never could force you away, and that in the event of war, you should have nothing to fear, as we would stand by and assist you."

He said that he had called at the prophet's lodge on his way down, and there had learned for the first time, that we had left our village. He informed me privately, that the prophet was anxious to see me, as he had much good news to tell me, and that I would hear good news in the spring from our British Father. "The prophet requested me to give you all the particulars, but I would much rather you would see him yourself and learn all from him. But I will tell you that he has received expresses from our British Father, who says that he is going to send us guns, ammunition, provisions and clothing early in the spring. The vessels that bring them will come by way of Milwaukee. The prophet has likewise received wampum and tobacco from the different nations on the lakes, Ottawas, Chippewas, and Pottowattomies, and as to the Winnebagoes he has them all at his command. We are going to be happy once more."

I told him I was pleased that our British Father intended to see us righted. That we had been driven from our lands without receiving anything for them, and I now began to hope from his talk, that my people would once more be happy. If I could accomplish this I would be satisfied. I am now growing old and could spend the remnant of my time anywhere. But I wish first to see my people happy. I can then leave them cheerfully. This has always been my constant aim, and I now begin to hope that our sky will soon be clear.

Neapope said:

"The prophet told me that all the tribes mentioned would fight for us if necessary, and the British father will support us. If we should be whipped, which is hardly possible, we will still be safe, the prophet having received a friendly talk from the chief of Wassicummico, at Selkirk's settlement, telling him, that if we were not happy in our own country, to let him know and he would make us happy. He had received information from our British father that we had been badly treated by the Americans. We must go and see the prophet. I will go first; you had better remain and get as many of your people to join you as you can. You know everything that we have done. We leave the matter with you to arrange among your people as you please. I will return to the prophet's village tomorrow. You can in the meantime make up your mind an to the course you will take and send word to the prophet by me, as he is anxious to assist us, and wishes to know whether you will join us, and assist to make your people happy."

During the night I thought over everything that Neapope had told me, and was pleased to think that by a little exertion on my part, I could accomplish the object of all my wishes. I determined to follow the advice of the prophet, and sent word by Neapope, that I would get all my braves together, explain everything that I had heard to them, and recruit as many as I could from the different villages.

Accordingly I sent word to Keokuk's band and the Fox tribe, explaining to them all the good news I had heard. They would not hear. Keokuk said that I had been imposed upon by liars, and had much better remain where I was and keep quiet. When he found that I was determined to make an attempt to recover my village, fearing that some difficulty would arise, he made application to the agent and great chief at St. Louis, asking permission for the chiefs of our nation to go to Washington to see our Great Father, that we might have our difficulties settled amicably. Keokuk also requested the trader, Colonel Davenport, who was going to Washington, to call on our Great Father and explain everything to him, and ask permission for us to come on and see him.

Having heard nothing favorable from the great chief at St. Louis, I concluded that I had better keep my band together, and recruit as many as possible, so that I would be prepared to make the attempt to rescue my village in the spring, provided our Great Father did not send word for us to go to Washington. The trader returned. He said he had called on our Great Father and made a full statement to him in relation to our difficulties, and had asked leave for us to go to Washington, but had received no answer.

I had determined to listen to the advice of my friends, and if permitted to go to see our Great Father, to abide by his counsel, whatever it might be. Every overture was made by Keokuk to prevent difficulty, and I anxiously hoped that something would be done for my people that it might be avoided. But there was bad management somewhere, or the difficulty that has taken place would have been avoided.

When it was ascertained that we would not be permitted to go to Washington, I resolved upon my course, and again tied to recruit some braves from Keookuk's band, to accompany me, but could not.

Conceiving that the peaceable disposition of Keokuk and his people had been in a great measure the cause of our having been driven from our village, I ascribed their present feelings to the same cause, and immediately went to work to recruit all my own band, and making preparations to ascend Rock river, I made my encampment on the Mississippi, where Fort Madison had stood. I requested my people to rendezvous at that place, sending out soldiers to bring in the warriors, and stationed my sentinels in a position to prevent any from moving off until all were ready.

My party having all come in and got ready, we commenced our march up the Mississippi; our women and children in canoes, carrying such provisions as we had, camp equipage, &c. My braves and warriors were on horseback, armed and equipped for defence. The prophet came down and joining us below Rock river, having called at Rock Island on his way down, to consult the war chief, agent and trader; who, he said, used many arguments to dissuade him from going with us, requesting him to come and meet us and turn us back. They told him also there was a war chief on his way to Rock Island with a large body of soldiers.

The prophet said he would not listen to this talk, because no war chief would dare molest us so long as we were at peace. That we had a right to go where we pleased peaceably, and advised me to say nothing to my braves and warriors until we encamped that night. We moved onward until we arrived at the place where General Gaines had made his encampment the year before, and encamped for the night. The prophet then addressed my braves and warriors. He told them to "follow us and act like braves, and we have nothing to fear and much to gain. The American war chief may come, but will not, nor dare not interfere with us so long as we act peaceably. We are not yet ready to act otherwise. We must wait until we ascend Rock river and receive our reinforcements, and we will then be able to withstand any army."

That night the White Beaver, General Atkinson, with a party of soldiers passed up in a steamboat. Our party became alarmed, expecting to meet the soldiers at Rock river, to prevent us going up. On our arrival at its mouth, we discovered that the steamboat had passed on.

I was fearful that the war chief had stationed his men on some high bluff, or in some ravine, that we might be taken by surprise. Consequently, on entering Rock river we commenced beating our drums and singing, to show the Americans that we were not afraid.

Having met with no opposition, we moved up Rock river leisurely for some distance, when we were overtaken by an express from White Beaver, with an order for me to return with my band and recross the Mississippi again. I sent him word that I would not, not recognizing his right to make such a demand, is I was acting peaceably, and intended to go to the prophet's village at his request, to make corn.

The express returned. We moved on and encamped some distance below the prophet's village. Here another express came from the White Beaver, threatening to pursue us and drive us back, if we did not return peaceably. This message roused the spirit of my band, and all were determined to remain with me and contest the ground with the war chief, should he come and attempt to drive us. We therefore directed the express to say to the war chief "if he wished to fight us he might come on." We were determined never to be driven, and equally so, not to make the first attack, our object being to act only on the defensive. This we conceived to be our right.

Soon after the express returned, Mr. Gratiot, sub-agent for the Winnebagoes, came to our encampment. He had no interpreter, and was compelled to talk through his chiefs. They said the object of his mission was to persuade us to return. But they advised us to go on— assuring us that the further we went up Rock river the more friends we would meet, and our situation would be bettered. They were on our side and all of their people were our friends. We must not give up, but continue to ascend Rock river, on which, in a short time, we would receive reinforcements sufficiently strong to repulse any enemy. They said they would go down with their agent, to ascertain the strength of the enemy, and then return and give us the news. They had to use some stratagem to deceive their agent in order to help us.

During this council several of my braves hoisted the British flag, mounted their horses and surrounded the council lodge. I discovered that the agent was very much frightened. I told one of his chiefs to tell him that he need not be alarmed, and then went out and directed my braves to desist. Every warrior immediately dismounted and returned to his lodge. After the council adjourned I placed a sentinel at the agent's lodge to guard him, fearing that some of my warriors might again frighten him. I had always thought he was a good man and was determined that he should not be hurt. He started with his chiefs to Rock Island.

Having ascertained that White Beaver would not permit us to remain where we were, I began to consider what was best to be done, and concluded to keep on up the river, see the Pottowattomies and have a talk with them. Several Winnebago chiefs were present, whom I advised of my intentions, as they did not seem disposed to render us any assistance. I asked them if they had not sent us wampum during the winter, and requested us to come and join their people and enjoy all the rights and privileges of their country. They did not deny this; and said if the white people did not interfere, they had no objection to our making corn this year, with our friend the prophet, but did not wish us to go any further up.

The next day I started with my party to Kishwacokee. That night I encamped a short distance above the prophet's village. After all was quiet in our camp I sent for my chiefs, and told them that we had been deceived. That all the fair promises that had been held out to us through Neapope were false. But it would not do to let our party know it. We must keep it secret among ourselves, move on to Kishwacokee, as if all was right, and say something on the way to encourage our people. I will then call on the Pottowattomies, hear what they say, and see what they will do.

We started the next morning, after telling our people that news had just come from Milwaukee that a chief of our British Father would be there in a few days. Finding that all our plans were defeated, I told the prophet that he must go with me, and we would see what could be done with the Pottowattomies. On our arrival at Kishwacokee an express was sent to the Pottowattomie villages. The next day a deputation arrived. I inquired if they had corn in their villages. They said they had a very little and could not spare any. I asked them different questions and received very unsatisfactory answers. This talk was in the presence of all my people. I afterwards spoke to them privately, and requested them to come to my lodge after my people had gone to sleep. They came and took seats. I asked them if they had received any news from the British on the lake. They said no. I inquired if they had heard that a chief of our British Father was coming to Milwaukee to bring us guns, ammunition, goods and provisions. They said no. I told them what news had been brought to me, and requested them to return to their village and tell the chiefs that I wished to see them and have a talk with them.

After this deputation started, I concluded to tell my people that if White Beaver came after us, we would go back, as it was useless to think of stopping or going on without more provisions and ammunition. I discovered that the Winnebagoes and Pottowattomies were not disposed to render us any assistance. The next day the Pottowattomie chiefs arrived in my camp. I had a dog killed, and made a feast. When it was ready, I spread my medicine bags, and the chiefs began to eat. When the ceremony was about ending, I received news that three or four hundred white men on horse-back had been seen about eight miles off. I immediately started three young men with a white flag to meet them and conduct them to our camp, that we might hold a council with them and descend Rock river again. I also directed them, in case the whites had encamped, to return, and I would go and see them. After this party had started I sent five young men to see what might take place. The first party went to the camp of the whites, and were taken prisoners. The last party had not proceeded far before they saw about twenty men coming toward them at full gallop. They stopped, and, finding that the whites were coming toward them in such a warlike attitude, they turned and retreated, but were pursued, and two of them overtaken and killed. The others then made their escape. When they came in with the news, I was preparing my flags to meet the war chief. The alarm was given. Nearly all my young men were absent ten miles away. I started with what I had left, about forty, and had proceeded but a short distance, before we saw a part of the army approaching. I raised a yell, saying to y braves, "Some of our people have been killed. Wantonly and cruelly murdered! We must avenge their death!"

In a little while we discovered the whole army coming towards us at a full gallop. We were now confident that our first party had been killed. I immediately placed my men behind a cluster of bushes, that we might have the first fire when they had approached close enough. They made a halt some distance from us. I gave another yell, and ordered my brave warriors to charge upon them, expecting that they would all be killed. They did charge. Every man rushed towards the enemy and fired, and they retreated in the utmost confusion and consternation before my little but brave band of warriors.

After following the enemy for some distance, I found it useless to pursue them further, as they rode so fast, and returned to the encampment with a few braves, as about twenty-five of them continued in pursuit of the flying enemy. I lighted my pipe and sat down to thank the Great Spirit for what he had done. I had not been meditating long, when two of the three young men I had seat with the flag to meet the American war chief, entered. My astonishment was not greater than my joy to see them living and well. I eagerly listened to their story, which was as follows:

"When we arrived near the encampment of the whites, a number of them rushed out to meet us, bringing their guns with them. They took us into their camp, where an American who spoke the Sac language a little told us that his chief wanted to know how we were, where we were going, where our camp was, and where was Black Hawk? We told him that we had come to see his chief, that our chief had directed us to conduct him to our camp, in case he had not encamped, and in that event to tell him that he, Black Hawk, would come to see him; he wished to hold a council with him, as he had given up all intention of going to war."

This man had once been a member of our tribe, having been adopted by me many years before and treated with the same kindness as was shown to our young men, but like the caged bird of the woods, he yearned for freedom, and after a few years residence with us an opportunity for escape came and he left us. On this occasion he would have respected our flag and carried back the message I had sent to his chief, had he not been taken prisoner, with a comrade, by some of my braves who did not recognize him, and brought him into camp. They were securely tied with cords to trees and left to meditate, but were occasionally buffeted by my young men when passing near them. When I passed by him there was a recognition on the part of us both, but on account of former friendship I concluded to let him go, and some little time before the sun went down I released him from his captivity by untying the cords that bound him and accompanied him outside of our lines so that he could escape safely. His companion had previously made a desperate effort to escape from his guards and was killed by them.

They continued their story:

"At the conclusion of this talk a party of white men came in on horseback. We saw by their countenances that something had happened. A general tumult arose. They looked at us with indignation, talked among themselves for a moment, when several of them cocked their guns and fired at us in the crowd. Our companion fell dead. We rushed through the crowd and made our escape. We remained in ambush but a short time, before we heard yelling like Indians running an enemy. In a little while we saw some of the whites in full speed. One of them came near us. I threw my tomahawk and struck him on the head which brought him to the ground; I ran to him and with his own knife took off his scalp. I took his gun, mounted his horse, and brought my friend here behind me. We turned to follow our braves, who were chasing the enemy, and had not gone far before we overtook a white man, whose horse had mired in a swamp. My friend alighted and tomahawked the man, who was apparently fast under his horse. He took his scalp, horse and gun. By this time our party was some distance ahead. We followed on and saw several white men lying dead on the way. After riding about six miles we met our party returning. We asked them how many of our men had been killed. They said none after the Americans had retreated. We inquired how many whites had been killed. They replied that they did not know, but said we will soon ascertain, as we must scalp them as we go back. On our return we found ten men, besides the two we had killed before we joined our friends. Seeing that they did not yet recognize us, it being dark, we again asked how many of our braves had been killed? They said five. We asked who they were? They replied that the first party of three who went out to meet the American war chief, had all been taken prisoners and killed in the encampment, and that out of a party of five, who followed to see the meeting of the first party with the whites, two had been killed. We were now certain that they did not recognize us, nor did we tell who we were until we arrived at our camp. The news of our death had reached it sometime before, and all were surprised to see us again."

The next morning I told the crier of my village to give notice that we must go and bury our dead. In a little while all were ready. A small deputation was sent for our absent warriors, and the remainder started to bury the dead. We first disposed of them and then commenced an examination in the enemy's deserted encampment for plunder. We found arms and ammunition and provisions, all of which we were sadly in want of, particularly the latter, as we were entirely without. We found also a variety of saddle bags, which I distributed among my braves, a small quantity of whisky and some little barrels that had contained this bad medicine, but they were empty. I was surprised to find that the whites carried whisky with them, as I had understood that all the pale faces, when acting is soldiers in the field, were strictly temperate.

The enemy's encampment was in a skirt of woods near a run, about half a day's travel from Dixon's ferry. We attacked them in the prairie, with a few bushes between us, about sundown, and I expected that my whole party would be killed. I never was so much surprised in all the fighting I have seen, knowing, too, that the Americans generally shoot well, as I was to see this army of several hundreds retreating, without showing fight, and passing immediately through their encampment, I did think they intended to halt there, as the situation would have forbidden attack by my party if their number had not exceeded half of mine, as we would have been compelled to take the open prairie whilst they could have picked trees to shield themselves from our fire.

I was never so much surprised in my life as I was in this attack. An army of three or four hundred men, after having learned that we were sueing for peace, to attempt to kill the flag bearers that had gone unarmed to ask for a meeting of the war chiefs of the two contending parties to hold a council, that I might return to the west side of the Mississippi, to come forward with a full determination to demolish the few braves I had with me, to retreat when they had ten to one, was unaccountable to me. It proved a different spirit from any I had ever before seen among the pale faces. I expected to see them fight as the Americans did with the British during the last war, but they had no such braves among them. At our feast with the Pottowattomies I was convinced that we had been imposed upon by those who had brought in reports of large re-enforcements to my band and resolved not to strike a blow; and in order to get permission from White Beaver to return and re-cross the Mississippi, I sent a flag of peace to the American war chief, who was reported to be close by with his army, expecting that he would convene a council and listen to what we had to say. But this chief, instead of pursuing that honorable and chivalric course, such as I have always practiced, shot down our flag-bearer and thus forced us into war with less than five hundred warriors to contend against three or four thousand soldiers.

The supplies that Neapope and the prophet told us about, and the reinforcements we were to have, were never more heard of, and it is but justice to our British Father to say were never promised, his chief being sent word in lieu of the lies that were brought to me, "for us to remain at peace as we could accomplish nothing but our own ruin by going to war."

What was now to be done? It was worse than folly to turn back and meet an enemy where the odds were so much against us and thereby sacrifice ourselves, our wives and children to the fury of an enemy who had murdered some of our brave and unarmed warriors when they were on a mission to sue for peace.

Having returned to our encampment, and found that all our young men had come in, I sent out spies to watch the movements of the army, and commenced moving up Kishwacokee with the balance of my people. I did not know where to go to find a place of safety for my women and children, but expected to find a good harbor about the head of Rock river. I concluded to go there, and thought my best route would be to go round the head of Kishwacokee, so that the Americans would have some difficulty if they attempted to follow us.

On arriving at the head of Kishwacokee, I was met by a party of Winnebagoes, who seemed to rejoice at our success. They said they had come to offer their services, and were anxious to join in. I asked them if they knew where there was a safe place for our women and children. They told us that they would send two old men with us to guide us to a good safe place.

I arranged war parties to send out in different directions, before I proceeded further. The Winnebagoes went alone. The war parties having all been fitted out and started, we commenced moving to the Four Lakes, the place where our guides were to conduct us. We had not gone far before six Winnebagoes came in with one scalp. They said they had killed a man at a grove, on the road from Dixon's to the lead mines. Four days after, the party of Winnebagoes who had gone out from the head of Kishwacokee, overtook us, and told me that they had killed four men and taken their scalps: and that one of them was Keokuk's father, (the agent). They proposed to have a dance over their scalps. I told them that I could have no dancing in my camp, in consequence of my having lost three young braves; but they might dance in their own camp, which they did. Two days after, we arrived in safety at the place where the Winnebagoes had directed us. In a few days a great number of our warriors came in. I called them all around me, and addressed them. I told them: "Now is the time, if any of you wish to come into distinction, and be honored with the medicine bag! Now is the time to show your courage and bravery, and avenge the murder of our three braves!"

Several small parties went out, and returned again in a few days, with success—bringing in provisions for our people. In the mean time, some spies came in, and reported that the army had fallen back to Dixon's ferry; and others brought news that the horsemen had broken up their camp, disbanded, and returned home.

Finding that all was safe, I made a dog feast, preparatory to leaving my camp with a large party, (as the enemy were stationed so far off).

Before my braves commenced feasting, I took my medicine bags, and addressed them in the following language:

"BRAVES AND WARRIORS: These are the medicine bags of our forefather, Mukataquet, who was the father of the Sac nation. They were handed down to the great war chief of our nation, Nanamakee, who has been at war with all the nations of the plains, and have never yet been disgraced! I expect you all to protect them!"

After the ceremony was over and our feasting done I started, with about two hundred warriors following my great medicine bags. I directed my course toward sunset and dreamed, the second night after we started, that there would be a great feast prepared for us after one day's travel. I told my warriors my dream in the morning and we started for Moscohocoynak, (Apple river). When we arrived in the vicinity of a fort the white people had built there we saw four men on horseback. One of my braves fired and wounded a man when the others set up a yell as if a large force were near and ready to come against us. We concealed ourselves and remained in this position for sometime watching to see the enemy approach, but none came. The four men, in the mean time, ran to the fort and gave the alarm. We followed them and attacked their fort. One of their braves, who seemed more valiant than the rest, raised his head above the picketing to fire at us when one of my braves, with a well-directed shot, put an end to his bravery. Finding that these people could not be killed without setting fire to their houses and fort I thought it more prudent to be content with what flour, provisions, cattle and horses we could find than to set fire to their buildings, as the light would be seen at a distance and the army might suppose we were in the neighborhood and come upon us with a strong force. Accordingly we opened a house and filled our bags with flour and provisions, took several horses and drove off some of their cattle.

We started in a direction toward sunrise. After marching a considerable time I discovered some white men coming towards us. I told my braves that we would go into the woods and kill them when they approached. We concealed ourselves until they came near enough and then commenced yelling and firing and made a rush upon them. About this time their chief, with a party of men, rushed up to rescue the men we had fired upon. In a little while they commenced retreating and left their chief and a few braves who seemed willing and anxious to fight. They acted like men, but were forced to give way when I rushed upon them with my braves. In a short time the chief returned with a lager party. He seemed determined to fight, and anxious for a battle. When he came near enough I raised the yell and firing commenced from both sides. The chief, who seemed to be a small man, addressed his warriors in a loud voice, but they soon retreated, leaving him and a few braves on the battle field. A great number of my warriors pursued the retreating party and killed a number of their horses as they ran.

The chief and his few braves were unwilling to leave the field. I ordered my braves to rush upon them, and had the mortification of seeing two of my chiefs killed before the enemy retreated.

This young chief deserves great praise for his courage and bravery, but fortunately for us, his army was not all composed of such brave men.

During this attack we killed several men and about forty horses and lost two young chiefs and seven warriors. My braves were anxious to pursue them to the fort, attack and burn it, but I told them it was useless to waste our powder as there was no possible chance of success if we did attack them, and that as we had ran the bear into his hole we would there leave him and return to our camp.

On arriving at our encampment we found that several of our spies had returned, bringing intelligence that the army had commenced moving. Another party of five came in and said they had been pursued for several hours, and were attacked by twenty-five or thirty whites in the woods; that the whites rushed in upon them as they lay concealed and received their fire without seeing them. They immediately retreated whilst we reloaded. They entered the thicket again and as soon as they came near enough we fired. Again they retreated and again they rushed into the thicket and fired. We returned their fire and a skirmish ensued between two of their men and one of ours, who was killed by having his throat cut. This was the only man we lost, the enemy having had three killed; they again retreated.

Another party of three Sacs had come in and brought two young white squaws, whom they had given to the Winnebagoes to take to the whites. They said they had joined a party of Pottowattomies and went with them as a war party against the settlers of Illinois.

The leader of this party, a Pottowattomie, had been severely whipped by this settler, sometime before, and was anxious to avenge the insult and injury. While the party was preparing to start, a young Pottowattomie went to the settler's house and told him to leave it, that a war party was coming to murder them. They started, but soon returned again, as it appeared that they were all there when the war party arrived.

The Pottowattomies killed the whole family, except two young squaws, whom the Sacs took up on their horses and carried off, to save their lives. They were brought to our encampment, and a messenger sent to the Winnebagoes, as they were friendly on both sides, to come and get them, and carry them to the whites. If these young men, belonging to my band, had not gone with the Pottowittomies, the two young squaws would have shared the same fate as their friends.

During our encampment at the Four Lakes we were hard pressed to obtain enough to eat to support nature. Situated in a swampy, marshy country, (which had been selected in consequence of the great difficulty required to gain access thereto,) there was but little game of any sort to be found, and fish were equally scarce. The great distance to any settlement, and the impossibility of bringing supplies therefrom, if any could have been obtained, deterred our young men from making further attempts. We were forced to dig roots and bark trees, to obtain something to satisfy hunger and keep us alive. Several of our old people became so reduced, as to actually die with hunger! Learning that the army had commenced moving, and fearing that they might come upon and surround our encampment, I concluded to remove our women and children across the Mississippi, that they might return to the Sac nation again. Accordingly, on the next day we commenced moving, with five Winnebagoes acting as our guides, intending to descend the Wisconsin.

Neapope, with a party of twenty, remained in our rear, to watch for the enemy, whilst we were proceeding to the Wisconsin, with our women and children. We arrived, and had commenced crossing over to an island, when we discovered a large body of the enemy coming towards us. We were now compelled to fight, or sacrifice our wives and children to the fury of the whites. I met them with fifty warriors, (having left the balance to assist our women and children in crossing) about a mile from the river, When an attack immediately commenced, I was mounted on a fine horse, and was pleased to see my warriors so brave. I addressed them in a load voice, telling them to stand their ground and never yield it to the enemy. At this time I was on the rise of a hill, where I wished to form my warriors, that we might have some advantage over the whites. But the enemy succeeded in gaining this point, which compelled us to fall into a deep ravine, from which we continued firing at them and they at us, until it began to grow dark. My horse having been wounded twice during this engagement, and fearing from his loss of blood that he would soon give out, and finding that the enemy would not come near enough to receive our fire, in the dusk of the evening, and knowing that our women and children had had sufficient time to reach the island in the Wisconsin, I ordered my warriors to return, by different routes, and meet me at the Wisconsin, and was astonished to find that the enemy were not disposed to pursue us.

In this skirmish with fifty braves, I defended and accomplished my passage over the Wisconsin, with a loss of only six men, though opposed by a host of mounted militia. I would not have fought there, but to gain time for our women and children to cross to an island. A warrior will duly appreciate the embarrassments I labored under—and whatever may be the sentiments of the white people in relation to this battle, my nation, though fallen, will award to me the reputation of a great brave in conducting it.

The loss of the enemy could not be ascertained by our party; but I am of the opinion that it was much greater, in proportion, than mine. We returned to the Wisconsin and crossed over to our people.

Here some of my people left me, and descended the Wisconsin, hoping to escape to the west side of the Mississippi, that they might return home. I had no objection to their leaving me, as my people were all in a desperate condition, being worn out with traveling and starving with hunger. Our only hope to save ourselves was to get across the Mississippi. But few of this party escaped. Unfortunately for them, a party of soldiers from Prairie du Chien were stationed on the Wisconsin, a short distance from its mouth, who fired upon our distressed people. Some were killed, others drowned, several taken prisoners, and the balance escaped to the woods and perished with hunger. Among this party were a great many women and children.

I was astonished to find that Neapope and his party of spies had not yet come in, they having been left in my rear to bring the news, if the enemy were discovered. It appeared, however, that the whites had come in a different direction and intercepted our trail but a short distance from the place where we first saw them, leaving our spies considerably in the rear. Neapope and one other retired to the Winnebago village, and there remained during the war. The balance of his party, being brave men, and considering our interests as their own, returned, and joined our ranks.

Myself and band having no means to descend the Wisconsin, I started over a rugged country, to go to the Mississippi, intending to cross it and return to my nation. Many of our people were compelled to go on foot, for want of horses, which, in consequence of their having had nothing to eat for a long time, caused our march to be very slow. At length we arrived at the Mississippi, having lost some of our old men and little children, who perished on the way with hunger.

We had been here but a little while before we saw a steamboat (the "Warrior,") coming. I told my braves not to shoot, as I intended going on board, so that we might save our women and children. I knew the captain (Throckmorton) and was determined to give myself up to him. I then sent for my white flag. While the messenger was gone, I took a small piece of white cotton and put it on a pole, and called to the captain of the boat, and told him to send his little canoe ashore and let me come aboard. The people on board asked whether we were Sacs or Winnebagoes. I told a Winnebago to tell them that we were Sacs, and wanted to give ourselves up! A Winnebago on the boat called out to us "to run and hide, that the whites were going to shoot!" About this time one of my braves had jumped into the river, bearing a white flag to the boat, when another sprang in after him and brought him to the shore. The firing then commenced from the boat, which was returned by my braves and continued for sometime. Very few of my people were hurt after the first fire, having succeeded in getting behind old logs and trees, which shielded them from the enemy's fire.

The Winnebago on the steamboat must either have misunderstood what was told, or did not tell it to the captain correctly; because I am confident he would not have allowed the soldiers to fire upon us if he had known my wishes. I have always considered him a good man, and too great a brave to fire upon an enemy when sueing for quarters.

After the boat left us, I told my people to cross if they could, and wished; that I intended going into the Chippewa country. Some commenced crossing, and such as had determined to follow them, remained; only three lodges going with me. Next morning, at daybreak, a young man overtook me, and said that all my party had determined to cross the Mississippi—that a number had already got over safely and that he had heard the white army last night within a few miles of them. I now began to fear that the whites would come up with my people and kill them before they could get across. I had determined to go and join the Chippewas; but reflecting that by this I could only save myself, I concluded to return, and die with my people, if the Great Spirit would not give us another victory. During our stay in the thicket, a party of whites came close by us, but passed on without discovering us.

Early in the morning a party of whites being in advance of the army, came upon our people, who were attempting to cross the Mississippi. They tried to give themselves up; the whites paid no attention to their entreaties, but commenced slaughtering them. In a little while the whole army arrived. Our braves, but few in number, finding that the enemy paid no regard to age or sex, and seeing that they were murdering helpless women and little children, determined to fight until they were killed. As many women as could, commenced swimming the Mississippi, with their children on their backs. A number of them were drowned, and some shot before they could reach the opposite shore.

One of my braves, who gave me this information, piled up some saddles before him, (when the fight commenced), to shield himself from the enemy's fire, and killed three white men. But seeing that the whites were coming too close to him, he crawled to the bank of the without being perceived, and hid himself under the bank until the enemy retired. He then came to me and told me what had been done. After hearing this sorrowful news, I started with my little party to the Winnebago village at Prairie La Cross. On my arrival there I entered the lodge of one of the chiefs, and told him that I wished him to go with me to his father, that I intended giving myself up to the American war chief and die, if the Great Spirit saw proper. He said he would go with me. I then took my medicine bag and addressed the chief. I told him that it was "the soul of the Sac nation—that it never had been dishonored in any battle, take it, it is my life—dearer than life—and give it to the American chief!" He said he would keep it, and take care of it, and if I was suffered to live, he would send it to me.

During my stay at the village, the squaws made me a white dress of deer skin. I then started with several Winnebagoes, and went to their agent, at Prairie du Chien, and gave myself up.

On my arrival there, I found to my sorrow, that a large body of Sioux had pursued and killed a number of our women and children, who had got safely across the Mississippi. The whites ought not to have permitted such conduct, and none but cowards would ever have been guilty of such cruelty, a habit which had always been practiced on our nation by the Sioux.

The massacre, which terminated the war, lasted about two hours. Our loss in killed was about sixty, besides a number that was drowned. The loss of the enemy could not be ascertained by my braves, exactly; but they think that they killed about sixteen during the action.

I was now given up by the agent to the commanding officer at Fort Crawford, the White Beaver having gone down the river. We remained here a short time, and then started for Jefferson Barracks, in a steam boat, under the charge of a young war chief, (Lieut. Jefferson Davis) who treated us all with much kindness. He is a good and brave young chief, with whose conduct I was much pleased. On our way down we called at Galena and remained a short time. The people crowded to the boat to see us: but the war chief would not permit them to enter the apartment where we were—knowing, from what his feelings would have been if he had been placed in a similar situation, that we did not wish to have a gaping crowd around us.

We passed Rock Island without stopping. The great war chief, Gen. Scott, who was then at Fort Armstrong, came out in a small boat to see us, but the captain of the steamboat would not allow anybody from the fort to come on board his boat, in consequence of the cholera raging among the soldiers. I did think that the captain ought to have permitted the war chief to come on board to see me, because I could see no danger to be apprehended by it. The war chief looked well, and I have since heard was constantly among his soldiers, who were sick and dying, administering to their wants, and had not caught the disease from them and I thought it absurd to think that any of the people on the steamboat could be afraid of catching the disease from a well man. But these people are not brave like war chiefs, who never fear anything.

On our way down, I surveyed the country that had cost us so much trouble, anxiety and blood, and that now caused me to be a prisoner of war. I reflected upon the ingratitude of the whites when I saw their fine houses, rich harvests and everything desirable around them; and recollected that all this land had been ours, for which I and my people had never received a dollar, and that the whites were not satisfied until they took our village and our graveyards from us and removed us across the Mississippi.

On our arrival at Jefferson Barracks we met the great war chief, White Beaver, who had commanded the American army against my little band. I felt the humiliation of my situation; a little while before I had been leader of my braves, now I was a prisoner of war, but had surrendered myself. He received us kindly and treated us well.

We were now confined to the barracks and forced to wear the ball and chain. This was extremely mortifying and altogether useless. Was the White Beaver afraid I would break out of his barracks and run away? Or was he ordered to inflict this punishment upon me? If I had taken him prisoner on the field of battle I would not have wounded his feelings so much by such treatment, knowing that a brave war chief would prefer death to dishonor. But I do not blame the White Beaver for the course he pursued, as it is the custom among the white soldiers, and I suppose was a part of his duty.

The time dragged heavily and gloomily along throughout the winter, although the White Beaver did everything is his power to render us comfortable. Having been accustomed, throughout a long life, to roam the forests o'er, to go and come at liberty, confinement, and under such circumstances, could not be less than torture.

We passed away the time making pipes until spring, when we were visited by the agent, trader and interpreter, from Rock Island, Keokuk and several chiefs and braves of our nation, and my wife and daughter. I was rejoiced to see the two latter and spent my time very agreeably with them and my people as long as they remained.

The trader, Sagenash, (Col. Davenport) presented me with some dried venison, which had been killed and cured by some of my friends. This was a valuable present, and although he had given me many before, none ever pleased me so much. This was the first meat I had eaten for a long time that reminded me of the former pleasures of my own wigwam, which had always been stored with plenty.

Keokuk and his chiefs, during their stay at the barracks, petitioned our Great Father, the president, to release us, and pledged themselves for our good conduct. I now began to hope I would soon be restored to liberty and the enjoyment of my family and friends, having heard that Keokuk stood high in the estimation of our Great Father, because he did not join me in the war, but I was soon disappointed in my hopes. An order came from our Great Father to the White Beaver to send us on to Washington.

In a little while all were ready and left Jefferson Barracks on board of a steamboat, under charge of a young war chief and one soldier, whom the White Beaver sent along as a guide to Washington. We were accompanied by Keokuk, wife and son, Appanooce, Wapello, Poweshiek, Pashippaho, Nashashuk, Saukee, Musquaukee, and our interpreter. Our principal traders, Col. Geo. Davenport, of Rock Island, and S. S. Phelps and clerk, William Cousland, of the Yellow Banks, also accompanied us. On our way up the Ohio we passed several large villages, the names of which were explained to me. The first is called Louisville, and is a very petty village, situated on the bank of the Ohio River. The next is Cincinnati, which stands on the bank of the same river. This is a large and beautiful village and seemed to be in a thriving condition. The people gathered on the bank as we passed, in great crowds, apparently anxious to see us.

On our arrival at Wheeling the streets and river banks were crowded with people, who flocked from every direction to see us. While we remained here many called upon us and treated us with kindness, no one offering to molest or misuse us. This village is not so large as either of those before mentioned, but is quite a pretty one.

We left the steamboat then, having traveled a long distance on the prettiest river I ever saw (except our Mississippi) and took the stage. Being unaccustomed to this mode of traveling, we soon got tired and wished ourselves seated in a canoe on one of our own rivers, that we might return to our friends. We had traveled but a short distance before our carriage turned over, from which I received a slight injury, and the soldier had one arm broken. I was sorry for this accident, as the young man had behaved well.

We had a rough and mountainous country for several days, but had a good trail for our carriage. It is astonishing what labor and pains the white people have had to make this road, as it passes over several mountains, which are generally covered with rocks and timber, yet it has been made smooth and easy to travel upon.

Rough and mountainous as this country is there are many wigwams and small villages standing on the roadside. I could see nothing in the country to induce the people to live in it, and was astonished to find so many whites living on the hills.

I have often thought of them since my return to my own people, and am happy to think that they prefer living in their own country to coming out to ours and driving us from it, as many of the whites have already done. I think with them, that wherever the Great Spirit places his people they ought to be satisfied to remain, and be thankful for what He has given them, and not drive others from the country He has given them because it happens to be better then theirs. This is contrary to our way of thinking, and from my intercourse with the whites, I have learned that one great principle of their religion is "to do unto others as you wish them to do unto you." Those people in the mountains seem to act upon this principle, but the settlers on our frontiers and on our lands seem never to think of it, if we are to judge by their actions.

The first village of importance that we came to, after leaving the mountains, is called Hagerstown. It is a large village to be so far from a river and is very pretty. The people appear to live well and enjoy themselves much.

We passed through several small villages on the way to Fredericktown, but I have forgotten their names. This last is a large and beautiful village. The people treated us well, as they did at all other villages where we stopped.

Here we came to another road much more wonderful than that through the mountains. They call it a railroad, (the Baltimore and Ohio). I examined it carefully, but need not describe it, as the whites know all about it. It is the most astonishing sight I ever saw. The great road over the mountains will bear no comparison to it, although it has given the white people much trouble to make. I was surprised to see so much money and labor expended to make a good road for easy traveling. I prefer riding horse back, however, to any other way, but suppose these people would not have gone to so much trouble and expense to make a road if they did not prefer riding in their new fashioned carriages, which seem to run without any trouble, being propelled by steam on the same principle that boats are on the river. They certainly deserve great praise for their industry.

On our arrival at Washington, we called to see our Great Father, the President. He looks as if he had seen as many winters as I have, and seems to be a great brave. I had very little talk with him, as he appeared to be busy and did not seem to be much disposed to talk. I think he is a good man; and although he talked but little, he treated us very well. His wigwam is well furnished with everything good and pretty, and is very strongly built.

He said he wished to know the cause of my going to war against his white children. I thought he ought to have known this before; and consequently said but little to him about it, as I expected he knew as well as I cold tell him.

He said he wanted us to go to Fortress Monroe and stay awhile with the war chief who commanded it. But having been so long from my people, I told him that I would rather return to my nation; that Keokuk had come here once on a visit to him, as we had done, and he had let him return again, as soon as he wished, and that I expected to be treated in the same manner. He insisted, however, on our going to Fortress Monroe; and as the interpreter then present could not understand enough of our language to interpret a speech, I concluded it was best to obey our Great Father, and say nothing contrary to his wishes.

During our stay at the city, we were called upon by many of the people, who treated us well, particularly the squaws; we visited the great council home of the Americans; the place where they keep their big guns; and all the public buildings, and then started for Fortress Monroe. The war chief met us on our arrival, and shook hands, and appeared glad to see me. He treated us with great friendship, and talked to me frequently. Previous to our leaving this fort, he made us a feast, and gave us some presents, which I intend to keep for his sake. He is a very good man and a great brave. I was sorry to leave him, although I was going to return to my people, because he had treated me like a brother, during all the time I remained with him.

Having got a new guide, a war chief (Maj. Garland), we started for our own country, taking a circuitous route. Our Great Father being about to pay a visit to his children in the big towns towards sunrise, and being desirous that we should have an opportunity of seeing them, had directed our guide to take us through.

On our arrival at Baltimore, we were much astonished to see so large a village; but the war chief told us we would soon see a larger one. This surprised us more. During our stay here, we visited all the public buildings and places of amusement, saw much to admire, and were well entertained by the people who crowded to see us. Our Great Father was there at the same time, and seemed to be much liked by his white children, who flocked around him, (as they had around us) to shake him by the hand. He did not remain long, having left the city before us. In an interview, while here, the President said:

"When I saw you in Washington, I told you that you had behaved very badly in going to war against the whites. Your conduct then compelled me to send my warriors against you, and your people were defeated with great loss, and several of you surrendered, to be kept until I should be satisfied that you would not try to do anymore injury. I told you, too, that I would inquire whether your people wished you to return, and whether, if you did return, there would be any danger to the frontier. Gen. Clark and Gen. Atkinson, whom you know, have informed me that your principal chief and the rest of your people are anxious you should return, and Keokuk has asked me to send you back. Your chiefs have pledged themselves for your good conduct, and I have given directions that you should be taken to your own country.

"Major Garland, who is with you, will conduct you through some of our towns. You will see the strength of the white people. You will see that our young men are as numerous as the leaves in the woods. What can you do against us? You may kill a few women and children, but such a force would seen be sent against you as would destroy your whole tribe. Let the red men hunt and take care of their families. I hope they will not again raise the tomahawk against their white brethren. We do not wish to injure you. We desire your prosperity and improvement. But if you again make war against our people, I shall send a force which will severely punish you. When you go back, listen to the councils of Keokuk and the other friendly chiefs; bury the tomahawk and live in peace with the people on the frontier. And I pray the Great Spirit to give you a smooth path and a fair sky to return."

I was pleased with our Great Father's talk and thanked him. Told him that the tomahawk had been buried so deep that it would never be resurrected, and that my remaining days would be spent in peace with all my white brethren.

We left Baltimore in a steamboat, and traveled in this way to the big village, where they make medals and money, (Philadelphia.) We again expressed surprise at finding this village so much larger than the one we had left; but the war chief again told us we would see another much larger than this. I had no idea that the white people had such large villages, and so many people. They were very kind to us, showed us all their great public works, their ships and steamboats. We visited the place where they make money, (the mint) and saw the men engaged at it. They presented each of us with a number of pieces of the coin as they fell from the mint, which are very handsome.

I witnessed a militia training in this city, in which were performed a number of singular military feats. The chiefs and men were all well dressed, and exhibited quite a warlike appearance. I think our system of military parade far better than that of the whites, but as I am now done going to war I will not describe it, or say anything more about war, or the preparations necessary for it.

We next started for New York, and on our arrival near the wharf, saw a large collection of people gathered at Castle Garden. We had seen many wonderful sights in our way—large villages, the great national road over the mountains, the railroad, steam carriages, ships, steamboat, and many other things; but we were now about to witness a sight more surprising than any of these. We were told that a man was going up in the air in a balloon. We watched with anxiety to see if this could be true; and to our utter astonishment, saw him ascend in the air until the eye could no longer perceive him. Our people were all surprised and one of our young men asked the Prophet if he was going up to see the Great Spirit?

After the ascension of the balloon, we landed and got into a carriage to go to the house that had been provided for our reception. We had proceeded but a short distance before the street was so crowded that it was impossible for the carriage to pass. The war chief then directed the coachman to take another street, and stop at a different house from the one we had intended. On our arrival here we were waited upon by a number of gentlemen, who seemed much pleased to see us. We were furnished with good rooms, good provisions, and everything necessary for our comfort.

The chiefs of this big village, being desirous that all their people should have an opportunity to see us, fitted up their great council home for this purpose, where we saw an immense number of people; all of whom treated us with great friendship, and many with great generosity. One of their great chiefs, John A. Graham, waited upon us and made a very pretty talk, which appeared in the village papers, one of which I now hand you.

Mr. Graham's Speech

"BROTHERS: OPEN YOUR EARS. YOU are brave men. You have fought like tigers, but in a bad cause. We have conquered you. We were sorry last year that you raised the tomahawk against us; but we believe you did not know us then as you do now. We think, in time to come, you will be wise, and that we shall be friends forever. You see that we are a great people, numerous as the flowers of the field, as the shells on the sea shore, or the fishes in the sea, We put one hand on the eastern, and at the same time the other on the western ocean. We all act together. If sometime our great men talk long and loud at our council fires, but shed one drop of white men's blood, our young warriors, as thick as the stars of the night, will leap aboard of our great boats, which fly on the waves and over the lakes—swift as the eagle in the air—then penetrate the woods, make the big guns thunder, and the whole heavens red with the flames of the dwellings of their enemies. Brothers, the President has made you a great talk. He has but one mouth. That one has sounded the sentiments of all the people. Listen to what he has said to you. Write it on your memories, it is good, very good.

"Black Hawk, take these jewels, a pair of topaz earrings, beautifully set in gold, for your wife or daughter, as a token of friendship, keeping always in mind, that women and children are the favorites of the Great Spirit. These jewels are from an old man, whose head is whitened with the snows of seventy winters, an old man who has thrown down his bow, put off his sword, and now stands leaning on his staff, waiting the commands of the Great Spirit. Look around you, see all this mighty people, then go to your homes, open your arms to receive your families. Tell them to buy the hatchet, to make bright the chain of friendship, to love the white men, and to live in peace with them, as long as the rivers run into the sea, and the sun rises and sets. If you do so, you will be happy. You will then insure the prosperity of unborn generations of your tribes, who will go hand in hand with the sons of the white men, and all shall be blessed by the Great Spirit. Peace and happiness by the blessing of the Great Spirit attend you. Farewell."

In reply to this fine talk, I said, "Brother: We like your talk. We like the white people. They are very kind to us. We shall not forget it. Your council is good. We shall attend to it. Your valuable present shall go to my squaw. We shall always be friends."

The chiefs were particular in showing us everything that they thought would be pleasing or gratifying to us. We went with them to Castle Garden to see the fire-works, which was quite an agreeable entertainment, but to the whites who witnessed it, less magnificent than would have been the sight of one of our large prairies when on fire.

We visited all the public buildings and places of amusement, which, to us, were truly astonishing yet very gratifying.

Everybody treated us with friendship, and many with great liberality. The squaws presented us many handsome little presents that are said to be valuable. They were very kind, very good, and very pretty—for pale-faces.

Among the men, who treated us with marked friendship, by the presentation of many valuable presents, I cannot omit to mention the name of my old friend Crooks, of the American Fur Company. I have known him long, and have always found him to be a good chief, one who gives good advice, and treats our people right. I shall always be proud to recognize him as a friend, and glad to shake him by the hand.

Being anxious to return to our people, our guide started with us for our own country. On arriving at Albany, the people were so anxious to see us, that they crowded the streets and wharfs, where the steamboats landed, so much, that it was almost impossible for us to pass to the hotel which had been provided for our reception. We remained here but a short time, it being a comparatively small village, with only a few large public buildings. The great council home of the state is located here, and the big chief (the governor) resides here, in an old mansion. From here we went to Buffalo, thence to Detroit, where I had spent many pleasant days, and anticipated, on my arrival, to meet many of my old friends, but in this I was disappointed. What could be the cause of this? Are they all dead? Or what has become of them? I did not see our old father them, who had always given me good advice and treated me with great friendship.

After leaving Detroit it was but a few days before we landed at Prairie du Chien. The war chief at the fort treated us very kindly, as did the people generally. I called on the agent of the Winnebagoes, (Gen. J. M. Street), to whom I had surrendered myself after the battle at Bad Axe, who received me very friendly. I told him that I had left my great medicine bag with his chiefs before I gave myself up; and now, that I was to enjoy my liberty again, I was anxious to get it, that I might head it down to my nation unsullied.

He said it was safe; he had heard his chiefs speak of it, and would get it and send it to me. I hope he will not forget his promise, as the whites generally do, because I have always heard that he was a good man, and a good father, and made no promise that he did not fulfill.

Passing down the Mississippi, I discovered a large collection of people in the mining country, on the west side of the river, and on the ground that we had given to our relation, Dubuque, a long time ago. I was surprised at this, As I had understood from our Great Father that the Mississippi was to be the dividing line between his red and white children, and he did not wish either to cross it. I was much pleased with this talk, and I knew it would be much better for both parties. I have since found the country much settled by the whites further down, and near to our people, on the west side of the river. I am very much afraid that in a few years they will begin to drive and abuse our people, as they have formerly done. I may not live to see it, but I feel certain the day is not far distant.

When we arrived at Rock Island, Keokuk and the other chiefs were sent for. They arrived the next day with a great number of their young men, and came over to see me. I was pleased to see them, and they all appeared glad to see me. Among them were some who had lost relations the year before. When we met, I perceived the tear of sorrow gush from their eyes at the recollection of their loss, yet they exhibited a smiling countenance, from the joy they felt at seeing me alive and well.

The next morning, the war chief, our guide, convened a council at Fort Armstrong. Keokuk and his party went to the fort; but, in consequence of the war chief not having called for me to accompany him, I concluded that I would wait until I was sent for. Consequently, the interpreter came and said, "they were ready, and had been waiting for me to come to the fort." I told him I was ready and would accompany him. On our arrival there the council commenced. The war chief said that the object of this council was to deliver me up to Keokuk. He then read a paper, and directed me to follow Keokuk's advice, and be governed by his counsel in all things! In this speech he said much that was mortifying to my feelings, and I made an indignant reply.

I do not know what object the war chief had in making such a speech; or whether he intended what he said; but I do know that it was uncalled for, and did not become him. I have addressed many war chiefs and listened to their speeches with pleasure, but never had my feelings of pride and honor insulted on any other occasion. But I am sorry I was so hasty in reply to this chief, because I said that which I did not intend.

In this council I met my old friend (Col. Wm. Davenport,) whom I had known about eighteen years. He is a good and brave chief. He always treated me well, and gave me good advice. He made me a speech on this occasion, very different from that of the other chief. It sounded like coming from a brave. He said he had known me a long time, that we had been good friends during that acquaintance, and, although he had fought against my braves, in our late war, he still extended the hand of friendship to me, and hoped that I was now satisfied, from what I had seen in my travels, that it was folly to think of going to war against the whites, and would ever remain at peace. He said he would be glad to see me at all times, and on all occasions would be happy to give me good advice.

If our Great Father were to make such men our agents he would much better subserve the interests of our people, as well as his own, than in any other way. The war chiefs all know our people, and are respected by them. If the war chiefs at the different military posts on the frontier were made agents, they could always prevent difficulties from arising among the Indians and whites; and I have no doubt, had the war chief above alluded to been our agent, we would never have had the difficulties with the whites we have had. Our agents ought always to be braves. I would, therefore, recommend to our Great Father the propriety of breaking up the present Indian establishment, and creating a new one, and make the commanding officers at the different frontier posts the agents of the Government for the different nations of Indians.

I have a good opinion of the American war chiefs generally with whom I am acquainted, and my people, who had an opportunity of seeing and becoming well acquainted with the great war chief (Gen. Winfield Scott), who made the last treaty with them, in conjunction with the great chief of Illinois (Governor Reynolds), all tell me that he is the greatest brave they ever saw, and a good man—one who fulfills his premises. Our braves spoke more highly of him than of any chief that had ever been among us, or made treaties with us. Whatever he says may be depended upon. If he had been our Great Father we never would have been compelled to join the British in the last war with America, and I have thought that as our Great Father is changed every few years, that his children would do well to put this great war chief in his place, for they cannot find a better chief for a Great Father anywhere.

I would be glad if the village criers (editors), in all the villages I passed through, would let their people know my wishes and opinions about this great war chief.

During my travels my opinions were asked for on different subjects, but for want of a good interpreter (our regular interpreter having gone home on a different route), were seldom given. Presuming that they would be equally acceptable now, I have thought it a part of my duty to lay the most important before the public.

The subject of colonizing the negroes was introduced and my opinion asked as to the best method of getting clear of these people. I was not fully prepared at that time to answer, as I knew but little about their situation. I have since made many inquiries on the subject, and find that a number of States admit no slaves, whilst the balance hold these negroes as slaves, and are anxious, but do not know how to get clear of them. I will now give my plan, which, when understood, I hope will be adopted.

Let the free States remove all the male negroes within their limits to the slave States; then let our Great Father buy all the female negroes in the slave States between the ages of twelve and twenty, and sell them to the people of the free States, for a term of years, say those under fifteen until they are twenty-one, and those of and over fifteen, for five years, and continue to buy all the females in the slave States as soon as they arrive at the age of twelve, and take them to the free States and dispose of them in the same way as the first, and it will not be long before the country is clear of the black-skins, about which I am told they have been talking for a long time, and for which they have expended a large amount of money.

I have no doubt but our Great Father would willingly do his part in accomplishing this object for his children, as he could not lose much by it, and would make them all happy. If the free States did not want them all for servants, we would take the balance in our nation to help our women make corn.

I have not time now, or is it necessary to enter more into detail about my travels through the United States. The white people know all about them, and my people have started to their hunting grounds and I am anxious to follow them.

Before I take leave of the public, I must contradict the story of some of the village criers, who, I have been told, accuse me of having murdered women ad children among the whites. This assertion is false! I never did, nor have I any knowledge that any of my nation ever killed a white woman or child. I make this statement of truth to satisfy the white people among whom I have been traveling, and by whom I have been treated with great kindness, that, when they shook me by the hand so cordially, they did not shake the hand that had ever been raised against any but warriors.

It has always been our custom to receive all strangers that come to our village or camps in time of peace on terms of friendship, to share with them the best provisions we have, and give them all the assistance in our power. If on a journey or lost, to put them on the right trail, and if in want of moccasins, to supply them. I feel grateful to the whites for the kind manner they treated me and my party whilst traveling among them, and from my heart I assure them that the white man will always be welcome in our village or camps, as a brother. The tomahawk is buried forever! We will forget what has passed, and may the watchword between the Americans and he Sacs and Foxes ever be—FRIENDSHIP.

I am done now. A few more moons and I must follow my fathers to the shades. May the Great Spirit keep our people and the whites always at peace, is the sincere wish of

BLACK HAWK

Starts for a New Home

After we had finished his autobiography the interpreter read it over to him carefully, and explained it thoroughly, so that he might make any needed corrections, by adding to, or taking from the narrations; but he did not desire to change it in any material matter. He said, "It contained nothing but the truth, and that it was his desire that the white people in the big villages he had visited should know how badly he had been treated, and the reason that had impelled him to act as he had done." Arrangements having been completed for moving to his new home, he left Rock Island on the 10th of October with his family and a small portion of his band, for his old hunting grounds on Skunk river, on the west side of the Mississippi river below Shokokon. Here he had a comfortable dwelling erected, and settled down with the expectation of making it his permanent home, thus spending the evening of his days in peace and quietude.

Our next meeting with the Chief was in the Autumn Of 1834 while on our way to the trading house of Captain William Phelps (now of Lewistown, Ills.), at Sweet Home, located on the bank of the Des Moines river. This was soon after the payment of the annuities at Rock Island, where the chiefs and head men had been assembled and received the money and divided it among their people by such rule as they saw fit to adopt; but this mode of distribution had proved very unsatisfactory to a large number of Indians who felt that they had been sorely wronged. The Sacs held a convocation at Phelps' trading house soon after our arrival, and petitioned their Great Father to change the mode of payment of their annuities. Black Hawk was a leading spirit in this movement, but thought best not to be present at the meeting. The writer of this drew up a petition in advance of the assembling of the meeting, in accordance with the views of the Messrs. Phelps, and after a short council, in which the Indians generally participated, the interpreter read and explained to them the petition, which was a simple prayer to their Great Father, to charge the mode of payment so that each head of a family should receive and receipt for his proportion of the annuity. They were all satisfied and the entire party "touched the goose quill," and their names were thus duly attached to this important document.

The Secretary of War had long favored this mode of payment of the annuities to the Indians, and at a meeting of the Cabinet to consider this petition the prayer of the Indians was granted, and in due time the Indian department received instructions, so that upon the payment of 1835 this rule was adopted. On his return from Rock Island, Black Hawk, with a number of his band, called on his old friend Wahwashenequa (Hawkeye), Mr. Stephen S. Phelps, to buy their necessary supplies for making a fall hunt, and to learn at what points trading houses would be established for the winter trade. During their stay the old chief had frequent interviews with the writer (his former amanuensis). He said he had a very comfortable home, a good corn field, and plenty of game, and had been well treated by the few whites who had settled in his neighborhood. He spent several days with us and then left for home with a good winter outfit.

The change in the manner of payment of annuities would have been opposed by Keokuk and his head men, had they been let into the secret, as the annuity money when paid over was principally controlled by him, and always to the detriment of the Sacs' traders who were in opposition to the American Fur Company, the former having to rely almost entirely upon the fall and winter trade in furs and peltries to pay the credits given the Indians before leaving for their hunts.

Black Hawk's Last Visit

To YELLOW BANKS WAS IN the fall of 1836, after the town of Oquawka had been laid out, and when told that the town had taken the Indian name, instead of its English interpretation, he was very much gratified, as he had known it as Oquawka ever since his earliest recollection and had always made it a stopping place when going out to their winter camps. He said the Skunk river country was dotted over with Cabins all the way down to the Des Moines river, and was filling up very fast by white people. A new village had been started at Shokokon (Flint Hills) by the whites, and some of its people have already built good houses, but the greater number are still living in log cabins. They should have retained its Indian name, Shokokon, as our people have spent many happy days in this village. Here too, we had our council house in which the braves of the Sac nation have many times assembled to listen to my words of counsel. It was situated in a secluded but romantic spot in the midst of the bluffs, not far from the river, and on frequent occasions, when it became necessary to send out parties to make war on the Sioux to redress our grievances, I have assembled my braves here to give them counsel before starting on he war-path. And here, too, we have often met when starting out in the fall for our fall and winter's hunt, to counsel in regard to our several locations for the winter. In those days the Fur Company had a trading house here and their only neighbors were the resident Indians of Tama's town, located a few miles above on the river.

The Burlington *Hawk-Eye*, of a late date, in reference to this council house, says:

"A little distance above the water works, and further around the turn of the bluff is a natural amphitheater, formed by the action of the little stream that for ages has dripped and gurgled down its deep and narrow channel to the river. It is a straight, clear cut opening in the hill side, slightly rising till at a distance of seventy-five or one hundred yards from the face of the bluff it terminates as suddenly and sharply as do the steeply sloping sides.

"Well back in this grassy retreat, upon a little projection of earth that elevates it above the surrounding surface, lies a huge granite boulder. In connection with the surroundings it gives to the place the appearance of a work of man, everything is so admirably arranged for a council chamber. Here, it is rumored by tradition, the dusky warriors of the Sacs gathered to listen in attentive silence to the words of their leader, Black Hawk, who from his rocky rostrum addressed the motionless groups that strewed the hill sides; motionless under his addresses and by them aroused to deeds of darkness and crafty daring that made the name of their chief a synonym with all things terrible.

"Whatever of truth this story may contain we cannot say, and it may be no one knows. Certain it is, however, that Black Hawk's early history is intimately linked and interwoven with that of our city, and in justice to a brave man and a soldier, as well as a 'first settler' and a citizen, his name and his last resting place should be rescued from the oblivion that will soon enshroud them."

Another village has been commenced by the whites on the Mississippi river, at Fort Madison, which is being built up very rapidly. The country, too, is fast settling up by farmers, and as the Sacs have made a settlement on the frontier farther west, on our old hunting grounds, he said he would have to move farther back so as to be near his people; and on bidding us farewell, said it might be the last time, as he was growing old, and the distance would be too great from the point at which he intended to build a house and open a little farm to make a visit on horseback, and as the Des Moines river is always low in the fall of the year he could not come in his canoe.

At the close of the summer of 1837 the President of the United States invited deputations from several tribes Of Indians residing on the Upper Mississippi to visit him at Washington. Among those who responded to his invitation were deputations from the Sacs and Foxes and Sioux, who had been at enmity, and between whom hostilities had been renewed, growing out of their inhuman treatment of many of the women and children of the Sacs, after they had made their escape from the battle of Bad Axe, at the close of the war.

Keokuk, principal chief of the Sacs and Foxes, (by the advice of his friend, Sagenash, Col. George Davenport, of Rock Island) invited Black Hawk to join his delegation, which invitation he readily accepted, and made one of the party; whilst the Sioux were represented by several of their crafty chiefs. Several counsels were held, the object of which was to establish peace between the Sacs and Foxes and Sioux, and in order to perpetuate it, make a purchase of a portion of the country of the Sioux, which territory should be declared neutral, and on which neither party should intrude for any purpose; but the Sioux, whose domain extends far and wide, would not consent to sell any of their land; hence nothing was accomplished.

Before returning to their county the Sac and Fox delegation visited the large cities in the East, in all of which Black Hawk attracted great attention; but more particularly in Boston, as he did not visit it during his former tour. The delegation embraced Keokuk, his wife and little son, four chiefs of the nation, Black Hawk and son, and several warriors. Here they were received and welcomed by the mayor of the city, and afterwards by Governor Everett as the representative of the State. On the part of the city, after a public reception, the doors of Faneuil Hall were opened to their visitors to hold a levee for the visits of the ladies, and in a very short time the "old cradle of liberty" was jammed full.

After dinner the delegation was escorted to the State House by a military company, and on their arrival were conspicuously seated in front of the Speakers' desk, the house being filled with ladies, members of the legislature, and dignitaries of the city council.

Governor Everett then addressed the audience, giving a brief history of the Sac and Fox tribe, whose principal chiefs (including the great war chief) were then present, and then turning to them hi said: "Chiefs and warriors of the united Sacs and Foxes, you are welcome to our hall of council. Brothers, you have come a long way from your home to visit your white brethren; we rejoice to take you by the hand. Brothers, we have heard the names of your chiefs and warriors. Our brethren who have traveled in the West have told us a great deal about the Sacs and Foxes. We rejoice to see you with our own eyes.

"Brothers, we are called the Massachusetts. This is the name of the red men who once lived here. Their wigwams were scattered on yonder fields, and their council fire was kindled on this spot. They were of the same great race as the Sacs and Foxes.

"Brothers, when our fathers came over the great water they were a small band. The red man stood upon the rock by the seaside and saw our fathers. He might have pushed them into the water and drowned them; but he stretched out his hand to them and said: 'Welcome, white man.' Our fathers were hungry, and the red man gave them corn and venison. They were cold, and the red man wrapped them in his blanket. We are now numerous and powerful, but we remember the kindness of the red men to our fathers. Brothers, you are welcome; we are glad to see you.

"Brothers, our faces are pale, and your faces are dark, but our hearts are alike. The Great Spirit has made His children of different colors, but He loves them all.

"Brothers, you dwell between the Mississippi and Missouri. They are mighty rivers. They have one branch far East in the Alleghanies and another far West in the Rocky Mountains, but they flow together at last into one great stream and ran down into the sea. In like manner the red man dwells in the West and the white man in the East, by the great water; but they are all one band, one family. It has many branches; but one head.

"Brothers, as you entered our council house, you beheld the image of our great father, Washington. It is a cold stone; it cannot speak to you, but he was the friend of the red man, and bade his children live in friendship with their red brethren. He is gone to the world of spirits, but his words have made a very deep print in our hearts, like the step of a strong buffalo on the soft clay of the prairie.

"Brother, (addressing Keokuk) I perceive your little son between your knees. May the Great Spirit preserve his life, my brother. He grows up before you, like the tender sapling by the side of the great oak. May they flourish for a long time together; and when the mighty oak is fallen on the ground may the young tree fill its place in the forest, and spread out its branches over the tribe.

"Brothers, I make you a short talk and again bid you welcome to our council hall."

Keokuk rose and made an eloquent address. Several of the other chiefs spoke, and after them the old war chief, Black Hawk, on whom the large crowd were looking with intense interest, arose and delivered a short but dignified address.

Presents were then distributed to them by the Governor. Keokuk received a splendid sword and a brace of pistols, his son a nice little rifle, the other chiefs long swords, and Black Hawk a sword and brace of pistols.

After the close of ceremonies in the Capitol, the Indians gave an exhibition of the war dance, in the common in front of the Capitol, in presence of thirty thousand spectators, and then returned to their quarters.

Black Hawk's Removal to the Des Moines River

Soon after his return from Boston he removed his family and little band farther West, on the Des Moines river, near the storehouse of an Indian trader, where he had previously erected a good house for his future home. His family embraced his wife, two sons, Nashashuk and Gamesett, and an only daughter and her husband. As he had given up the chase entirely—having sufficient means from the annuities—he now turned his attention to the improvement of his grounds, and soon had everything comfortably around him. Here he had frequent visits from the whites, who came out in large numbers to look at the country, many of whom called through curiosity to see the great war chief, but all were made welcome and treated with great hospitality.

In 1838 Fort Madison had grown to be a little village, and its inhabitants were not only enterprising and industrious, but patriotic citizens. On the 4th of July of that year they had a celebration and having known and respected Black Hawk while residing in that part of the country, invited him to join them as a guest on that occasion.

In reply to a letter of B.F. Drake, Esq., of Cincinnati, asking for such incidents in the life of Black Hawk as he knew, Hon. W. Henry Starr, of Burlington, Iowa, whom we knew for many years as a highly honorable and intelligent gentleman, gave the following account of the celebration in his reply, dated March 21, 1839:

"On the 4th of July, 1838, Black Hawk was present by special invitation, and was the most conspicuous guest of the citizens assembled in commemoration of that day. Among the toasts called forth by the occasion was the following:

"'Our illustrious guest, Black Hawk: May his declining years be as calm and serene as his previous life has been boisterous and full of warlike incidents. His attachment and great friendship to his white brethren, fully entitle him to a seat at our festive board.'"

"So soon as this sentiment was drank, Black Hawk arose and delivered the following speech, which was taken down at the time by two interpreted, and by them furnished for publication:

"It has pleased the Great Spirit that I am here today. I have eaten with my white friends. The earth is our mother—we are now on it—with the Great Spirit above us—it is good. I hope we are all friends here. A few summers ago I was fighting against you—I did wrong, perhaps; but that is past—it is buried—let it be forgotten.

"Rock river was a beautiful country—liked my towns, my cornfields, and the home of my people. I fought for it. It is now yours—keep it as we did—it will produce you good crops.

"I thank the Great Spirit that I am now friendly with my white brethren—we are here together—we have eaten together—we are friends—it is his wish and mine. I thank you for your friendship.

"I was once a great warrior-I am now poor. Keokuk has been the cause of my present situation—but do not attach blame to him. I am now old. I have looked upon the Mississippi since I have been a child. I love the Great river. I have dwelt upon its banks from the time I was an infant. I look upon it now. I shake hands with you, and as it is my wish, I hope you are my friends.'

"In the course of the day he was prevailed upon to drink several times, and became somewhat intoxicated, an uncommon circumstance, as he was generally temperate.

"In the autumn of 1837, he was at the house of an Indian trader, in the vicinity of Burlington, when I became acquainted and frequently convened with him in broken English, and through the medium of gestures and pantomine. A deep seated melancholy was apparent in his countenance, and conversation. He endeavored to make me comprehend, on one occasion, his former greatness, and represented that he was once master of the country, east, north, and south of us—that he had been a very successful warrior-called himself, smiting his breast, 'big Captain Black Hawk,' 'nesso Kaskaskias,' (killed the Kaskaskias,) 'nesso Sioux a heap,' (killed a great number of Sioux). He then adverted to the ingratitude of his tribe, in permitting Keokuk to supercede him, who, he averred, excelled him in nothing but drinking whisky.

"Toward Keokuk he felt the most unrelenting hatred. Keokuk was, however, beyond his influence, being recognized as chief of the tribe by the government of the United States. He unquestionably possessed talents of the first order, excelled as an orator, but his authority will probably be short-lived, on account of his dissipation and his profligacy in spending the money paid him for the benefit of his tribe, and which he squanders upon himself and a few favorites, through whose influence he seeks to maintain his authority.

"You inquire if Black Hawk was at the battle of the Thames? On one occasion I mentioned Tecumthe to him and he expressed the greatest joy that I had heard of him, and pointing away to the East, and making a feint, as if aiming a gun, said, 'Chemocoman (white man) nesso,' (kill.) From which I had no doubt of his being personally acquainted with Tecumthe, and I have been since informed, on good authority, that he was in the battle of the Thames and in several other engagements with that distinguished chief."

In September, 1838, he started with the head men of his little band to go to Rock Island, the place designated by the Agent, to receive their annuities, but was taken sick on the way and had to return to his home. He was confined to his bed about two weeks, and on the 3d day of October, 1838, he was called away by the Great Spirit to take up his abode in the happy grounds of the future, at the age of seventy-one years. His devoted wife and family were his only and constant attendants during his last sickness, and when brought home sick, she had a premonition that he would soon be called away.

The following account of his death and burial we take from the Burlington Hawk-Eye, and as we knew the writer as a reliable gentleman, many years ago, we have no doubt of it being strictly correct.

Captain James H. Jordan, a trader among the Sacs and Foxes before Black Hawk's death, was present at his burial, and is now residing on the very spot where he died. In reply to a letter of inquiry he writes as follows:

ELDON, Iowa, July 15, 1881

Black Hawk was buried on the northeast quarter of the southeast quarter of section 2, township 70, range 12, Davis county, Iowa, near the northeast corner of the county, on the Des Moines river bottom, about ninety rods from where he lived when he died, and the north side of the river. I have the ground on which he lived for a door yard, it being between my house and the river. The only mound over the gave was some puncheons split out and set over his grave and then sodded over with blue gross, making a ridge about four feet high. A flag-staff, some twenty feet high, was planted at the head, on which was a silk flag, which hung there until the wind wore it out. My house and his were only about four rods apart when he died. He was sick only about fourteen days. He was buried right where he sat the year before, when in council with Iowa Indians, and was buried in a suit of military clothes, made to order and given to him when in Washington City by General Jackson, with hat, sword, gold epaulets, etc., etc.

The Annals of Iowa of 1863 and 1864 state that the old chief was buried by laying his body on a board, his feet fifteen inches below the surface of the ground, and his head raised three feet above the ground. He was dressed in a military uniform, said to have been presented to him by a member of General Jackson's cabinet, with a cap on his head ornamented with feathers. On his left side was a sword presented him by General Jackson; on his right side a cane presented to him by Henry Clay, and one given to him by a British officer, and other trophies. Three medals hung about his neck from President Jackson, ex-President John Quincy Adams and the city of Boston, respectively. The body was covered with boards on each side, the length of the body, which formed a ridge, with an open space below; the gables being closed by boards, and the whole was covered with sod. At the head was a flag-staff thirty-five feet high which bore an American flag worn out by exposure, and near by was the usual hewn post inscribed with Indian characters representing his war-like exploits, etc. Enclosing all was a strong circular picket fence twelve feet high. His body remained here until July, 1839, when it was carried off by a certain Dr. Turner, then living at Lexington, Van Buren county, Iowa. Captain Horn says the bones were carried to Alton, Ills., to be mounted with wire. Mr. Barrows says they were taken to Warsaw, Ills. Black Hawk's sons, when they heard of this desecration of their father's grave, were very indignant, and complained of it to Governor Lucas of Iowa Territory, and his excellency caused the bones to be brought back to Burlington in the fall of 1839, or the spring of 1840. When the sons came to take possession of them, finding them safely stored "in a good dry place" they left them there. The bones were subsequently placed in the collection of the Burlington Geological and Historical Society, and it is certain that they perished in the fire which destroyed the building and all the society's collections in 1855; though the editor of the Annals, (April, 1865, p. 478) says there is good reason to believe that the bones were not destroyed by the fire, and he is "creditably informed that they are now at the residence of a former officer of said society and thus escaped that catastrophe."

Another account, however, and probably a more reliable one, states that the last remains of Black Hawk were consumed as stated, in the burning building containing the collections and properties of the Burlington Geological and Historical Society.

In closing this narrative of the life of this noble old chief it may be but just to speak briefly of his personal traits. He was an Indian, and from that standpoint we must judge him. The make-up of his character comprised those elements in a marked degree which constitutes a noble nature. In all the social relations of life he was kind and affable. In his house he was the affectionate husband and father. He was free from the many vices that others of his race had contracted from their associations with the white people, never using intoxicating beverages to excess. As a warrior he knew no fear, and on the field of battle his feats of personal prowess stamped him as the "bravest of the brave."

But it was rather as a speaker and counsellor that he was distinguished. His patriotism, his love of his country, his home, his lands and the rights of his people to their wide domain, moved his great soul to take up arms to protect the rights of his people. Revenge and conquest formed no part of his purpose. *Right* was all that he demanded, and for *that* he waged the unequal contests with the whites. With his tribe he had great personal influence and his young men received his counsel and advice, and yielded ready acquiescence in his admonitions. With other tribes he was held in high esteem, as well as by English and American soldiers, who had witnessed his prowess on the field of battle.

The Black Hawk Tower

THIS FAVORITE RESORT OF BLACK Hawk, situated on the highest bank of Rock river, had been selected by his father as a lookout, at the first building up of their village. From this point they had an unobstructed view up and down Rock river for many miles, and across the prairies as far as the vision could penetrate, and since that country has been settled by the whites, for more than half a century, has been the admiration of many thousands of people.

The village of Black Hawk, including this grand "look out," was purchased from the Government by Col. George Davenport, at Black Hawk's particular request, for the reason, as he afterwards told us, that he could leave it with an abiding assurance that the graves of their people would be protected from vandal hands.

This property including hundreds of acres lying between Rock river and the Mississippi, is now owned by Hon. B. Davenport, and as it has long been a pleasure resort for picnic and other parties, he has erected an elegant pavilion on its site, with a good residence for a family, who have charge of it, which will now make it the finest pleasure resort in that part of the country. And in order to make it more easy of access, he has constructed a branch from the Rock Island and Milan railroad, leading directly to the Tower. Now its many visitors in the future can sit on the veranda, and while enjoying the elegant scenery, can take ease and comfort in the cool shade. And for this high privilege the name of Davenport will receive many hearty greetings.

Fifty years ago (1832) we made, our first visit to Black Hawk's Tower with Col. George Davenport, and listened with intense interest to his recital of scenes that had been enacted there may years before; and one year later had them all repeated, with may more, from the lips of Black Hawk himself. How changed the scene. Then it was in its rustic state, now this fine pavilion, being a long, low structure, built somewhat after the Swiss cottage plan, with broad sloping roofs, and wide, long porches on the north and south sides, the one facing the road and the other fronting the river and giving a view of a beautiful stretch of country up and down Rock river, greatly enhances its beauty and adds much to the comfort of visitors.

The following beautiful word paintings by a recent visitor to the Tower, we take from the Rock Island Union:

BLACK HAWK'S WATCH TOWER

BY JENNIE M. FOWLER

Beautiful tower! famous in history
Rich in legend, in old-time mystery,
Graced with tales of Indian lore,
Crowned with beauty from summit to shore.

Below, winds the river, silent and still,
Nestling so calmly 'mid island and hill,
Above, like warriors, proudly and grand,
Tower the forest trees, monarchs of land.

A land mark for all to admire and wonder,
With thy history ancient, for nations to ponder,
Boldly thou liftest they head to the breeze,
Crowned with they plumes, the nodding trees.

Years are now gone—forever more fled,
Since the Indians crept, with cat-like tread,
With mocasined foot, with eagle eye—
The red men our foes in ambush lie.

The owl, still his nightly vigil keeps,
While the river, below him, peacefully sleeps,
The whip-poor-will utters his plaintive cry,
The trees still whisper, and gently sigh.

The pale moon still creeps from her daily rest,
Throwing her rays o'er the river's dark breast,
The katy-did and cricket, I trow,
In days gone by, chirruped, even as now.

Indian! thy camp-fires no longer are smoldering,
They bones 'neath the forest moss long have been mouldering,
The "Great Spirit" claims thee. He leadeth they tribe,
To new hunting-grounds not won with a bribe.

On thy Watch Tow'r the pale face his home now makes,
His dwelling, the site of the forest tree takes,
Gone are thy wigwams, the wild deer now fled,
Black Hawk, with his tribe, lie silent and dead.

ROCK ISLAND, August 18, 1882

THE BLACK HAWK WAR

PREFACE

On the 12th of April, 1832, soon after our arrival at Rock Island on a visit to relatives, (the family of Col. Geo. Davenport) a steamboat came down from Galena with officers to Fort Armstrong, for the purpose of laying in supplies and medical stores for a brigade then being formed at that place. One regiment, composed principally of miners, who had abandoned their mines and came in to offer their services as soldiers in the field, were unanimous in the election of Henry Dodge as Colonel. They had long known him as a worthy, brave and accomplished gentleman, the soul of honor, and hence would be an intrepid soldier.

Among the officers on this trip was Dr. A. K. Philleo, well known to Col. Dodge as a social gentleman, a skilled physician and an accomplished surgeon, who had accepted the position of surgeon at his urgent request, with a *proviso:* Being editor of the *Galenian,* (the only paper printed in the town) he considered the position a very important one, as it was the only paper within hundreds of miles of the seat of war, and the only one on the Mississippi above Alton, Ill.; hence he must procure a substitute or decline the appointment of surgeon. Having made his acquaintance after he had learned that we had been engaged in newspaper life, he insisted that we should take a position on the *Galenian* for a few weeks, or until the close of the war, so that he could accept the offer of Col. Dodge, and seeing that he was a great favorite among the officers, and anxious to go to the field, we accepted the position and accompanied him to Galena the same evening.

Here we found an infantry regiment, commanded by Col. J.M. Strode, composed principally of miners and citizens of Galena, which had been hurriedly organized for home protection, whilst that of Col. Dodge, being well mounted, were making preparations to take the field. After taking charge of the *Galenian* we made the acquaintance of Col. Strode, and found him to be a whole-souled Kentuckian, who advised us to enroll our name on the company list of Capt. M. M. Maughs, and as our time would mostly be devoted to the paper, he would detail us *Printer to the Regiment,* by virtue of which appointment we would become an honorary member of his staff. We retained our position on the paper and that on the staff of the Colonel throughout the war, and was made the recipient of dispatches of the regular movement of the army, its skirmishes and battles from officers of the regular army as well as that of the volunteers, from which we made our weekly report, and from these data we have made up most of our history of the war.

Fox Murderers Wanted

E arly in April, 1832, Brig.-General Atkinson, with about three hundred troops, was ordered to Fort Armstrong to prevent a threatened war between the Menominees and Fox Indians, on account of a massacre, committed by a band of the latter on a small band of drunken Menominees the previous summer at a point near Fort Crawford. To prevent bloodshed he was directed to demand the murderers of the Foxes; but on arriving at Rock Island he soon learned that there was imminent danger of a war of a different character—that Black Hawk, with his entire band, was then on his way to invade the State of Illinois and would probably be joined by the Pottowattamies and Winnebagoes. In order to ascertain the facts in the case, he called upon the Indian Agent and Col. George Davenport, both located here, and requested them to furnish, in writing, all the information they had in relation to the movements and intentions of Black Hawk in coming to the State of Illinois. Both gentlemen replied to his inquiries immediately as follows:

Rock Island, April 12, 1832

My opinion is that the squaws and old men have gone to the Prophet's town, on Rock river, and the warriors are now only a few miles below the mouth of Rock river, within the limits of the State of Illinois. That these Indians are hostile to the whites there is no doubt. That they have invaded the State of Illinois, to the great injury of her citizens, is equally true. Hence it is that that the public good requires that strong as well as speedy measures should be taken against Black Hawk and his followers.

Respectfully, I have the honor to be your obedient servant,
(Signed,) Andrew S. Hughes
To Brig-Gen. Atkinson

Rock Island, April 13, 1832

Dear Sir

In reply to your inquiry of this morning, respecting the Indians, I have to state that I have been informed by the man I have wintering with the Indians that the British band of Sac Indians are determined to make war upon the frontier settlements. The British band of Sac Indians did rendezvous at old Fort Madison, and induced a great many of the young men to join them on their arrival at the Yellow Banks. They crossed about five hundred head of horses into the State of Illinois, and sent about seventy horses through the country toward Rock River. The remainder, some on horseback the others in canoes, in a fighting order, advanced up the Mississippi, and were encamped yesterday five or six miles below Rock river and will no doubt endeavor to reach their stronghold in the Rock river swamps if they are not intercepted. From every information that I have received, I am of the opinion that the intentions of the British band of Sac Indians is to commit depredations on the inhabitants of the frontier."

Respectfully, your obedient servant,
GEORGE DAVENPORT. (Signed,)
To Brig. Gen. Atkinson

Being satisfied from the information thus acquired, that there was danger ahead for the small settlements of whites in the Northern portion of the State, he immediately addressed a letter to Gov. Reynolds, of Illinois, from which we take the following:

FORT ARMSTRONG, April 13, 1832

DEAR SIR

The band of Sacs, under Black Hawk, joined by about one hundred Kickapoos and a few Pottowattomies, amounting in all to about five hundred men, have assumed a hostile attitude. They crossed the river at the Yellow, Banks on the sixth inst., and are now moving up on the east side of Rock river, towards the Prophet's village.

"The regular force under my command is too small to justify me in pursuing the hostile party. To make an unsuccessful attempt to coerce them would only irritate them to acts of hostility on the frontier sooner than they probably contemplate.

"Your own knowledge of the character of these Indians, with the information herewith submitted, will enable you to judge of the course proper to pursue. I think the frontier is in great danger, and will use all the means at my disposal to co-operate with you in its protection and defense. With great respect,

Your most obedient servant,
H. ATKINSON,
Brigadier General of the U. S. Army,
His Excellency, Gov. Reynolds, Belleville, Ills.

On receipt of Gen. Atkinson's letter, Gov. Reynolds issued his proclamation, calling out a strong detachment of militia to rendezvous at Beardstown on the 22d of April. In obedience to this command a large number of citizens assembled and offered their services. They were met by Gov. Reynolds, and after bring organized into a brigade, he appointed Brig. Gen. Samuel Whitesides commander. His brigade embraced 1600 horsemen and two hundred footmen—being four regiments and an odd spy battalion.

First regiment, Col. Dewitt; second, Col. Fry; third, Col. Thomas; fourth, Col. Thompson; Col. James D. Henry, commanded the spy battalion.

The troops took up their line of march at once, under command of Gen. Whitesides, accompanied by the Commander-in-Chief, Gov. Reynolds. For the purpose of laying in provisions for the campaign they went to Yellow Banks, on the Mississippi river, where Major S. S. Phelps, who had been appointed quarter master, supplied them. They arrived on the 3d of May, and left for Rock river on the 7th.

The Black Hawk War

About the first of April Black Hawk's band assembled at Fort Madison for the purpose of making arrangements to ascend the Mississippi, and soon after the entire party started. The old men, women and children, with their provisions and camp equipage, in canoes, and the men all armed, came on horseback. On the sixth day of April, the braves, on horseback, made a call at Yellow Banks, one day after the canoes had passed the same point, and told Josiah Smart, Mr. Phelps' interpreter, where they were going, and the object of their visit. They said they had observed a great war chief, with a number of troops going up on a steamboat, and thought it likely that the mission of this war chief was to prevent them going up Rock river, but they were bound to go. Messrs. Phelps and Smart tried to persuade them to recross the river and return to their country, assuring them that the Government would not permit them to come into Illinois in violation of the treaty they had made last year, in which they had agreed to remain on the west side of the river. But they would not listen to their advice. On the next day they took up the line of march for Rock river, and on the 10th of April, 1832, Black Hawk, with a portion of his band of Sacs, reached the mouth of Rock river a few miles below Rock Island. The old men, women and children with their provisions and camp equipage, who came up in canoes, arrived on the 9th, and the men all armed, came up on horseback, reaching the camp on the 10th. While encamped there they were joined by the Prophet, who had previously invited them to come up to the country of the Winnebagoes and raise a crop. He called on his way at Fort Armstrong and had talks with the Agent and Col. Davenport, the trader, both of whom advised him to persuade Black Hawk and party to return to their own country, or they would be driven back by the soldiers then at Fort Armstrong, under the command of Gen. Atkinson, who had just arrived. The Prophet would not listen to their advice, but assured Black Hawk that he had a right to go forward with his entire party to the Winnebago country; and as he expected large reinforcements to his little army as he ascended Rock river, he was determined to go forward, but had given positive orders to his band, under no circumstances, to strike a blow until they had been reinforced by warriors from the Winnebagoes and Pottowattomies.

Early next morning they broke camp and started up Rock river, but were soon overtaken by a small detachment of soldiers, who held a council with Black Hawk and communicated to him the orders of Gen. Atkinson. These were for him to return with his band and re-cross the Mississippi. Black Hawk said, as he was not on the war path, but going on a friendly visit to the Prophet's village, he intended to go forward, and continued on his journey. On receipt of his answer, Gen. Atkinson sent another detachment to Black Hawk with imperative orders for him to return, or he would pursue him with his entire army and drive him back. In reply, Black Hawk said the General had no right to make the order so long as his band was peaceable, and that he intended to go on to the Prophet's village.

In the meantime the forces under the command of Gen. Whitesides had arrived, and were turned over to Gen. Atkinson by the Governor. The brigade, under the command of Gen. Whitesides, was ordered up Rock river to Dixon's Ferry, and as soon as boats could be got ready, Gen. Atkinson started for the same destination with 300 regulars and about the same number of Illinois militia. Black Hawk with his party had already reached a point some thirty or forty miles above Dixon's Ferry, where they were met in council by some Pottowattomies and Winnebago chiefs. They assured Black Hawk that their people would not join him in making war against the United States, and denied the Prophet's story to him. During this council Black Hawk became convinced that he had been badly imposed upon by the Prophet, and resolved at once to send a flag of truce to Gen. Atkinson and ask permission to descend Rock river, re-cross the Mississippi and go back to their country.

Stillman's Defeat

ABOUT THIS TIME, GEN. WHITESIDES had concentrated a large force of militia at Dixon's Ferry, and at the solicitation of Major Stillman, permitted him to take out a scouting party of nearly 300 mounted men. They went up Rock river, about thirty miles to Sycamore creek, and encamped within a few miles of Black Hawk's camp, but were not aware of its position at the time. Indian scouts having intercepted their coming reported at once to Black Hawk that a large army of mounted militia were coming towards his camp; and before the volunteers had entirely completed their arrangements for encampment, outside guards espied three Indians coming in with a white flag. After holding a parley with them, (one of the guards being able to talk a little with them in their own language), they were hurried into camp, and before any explanations were made, the flag bearer was shot and instantly killed, whilst his comrades made their escape during the confusion in getting the regiment ready to pursue the fleeing Indians. These had secreted themselves in ambush as the army rushed by, helter skelter, after another small party of Indians who had followed the flag bearers, and who, when hearing the uproar in camp made a hasty retreat. The entire regiment was soon mounted and started out in squads towards the camp of Black Hawk. The latter having learned by a scout that the army was coming, started at once with less than fifty mounted warriors, his entire force then in camp, to meet the enemy, and on arriving at a copse of timber and underbrush near Sycamore creek, made ready to meet them.

Capt. Eads' company, who were the first to start out, killed two of the five fleeing Indians. Soon after crossing Sycamore creek they were surprised by a terrific war whoop from the Indians, who were concealed in the bushes near by, and with deadly aim commenced firing into the front ranks of the regiment, and with unearthly yells (as one of the fleeing party told us on arriving at Galena), charged upon our ranks, with tomahawks raised, ready to slaughter all who might come within their reach. Judging from the yelling of the Indians, their number was variously estimated at from one thousand to two thousand.

The entire party was thrown into such confusion that Major Stillman had no control of any of them, and, with one exception, the entire army continued their flight to Dixon's Ferry, thirty miles distant, whilst some went back to their homes.

The retreating army passed through their camping ground near Sycamore creek, where they should have halted, and under cover of the timber, could have shot down their pursuers while yet in open prairie. Black Hawk and a small portion of his command gave up the chase, and returned to his camp, while the remainder pursued the fugitives for several miles, occasionally overtaking and killing some soldiers, whose horses had given out.

Among the retreating party was a Methodist preacher, whose horse was too slow to keep out of the reach of the Indians, who adopted a novel plan to save himself and horse. On coming to a ravine he left the track of his pursuers name distance, and followed down the ravine until he found a place deep enough to shelter himself and horse from view, and remained there for two hours in safety. He had the precaution to keep a strict count of the Indians as they went forward, and waited their return. Being satisfied that all had returned and continued on the way to their camp, he quietly left his hiding place, trotted leisurely along and reached Dixon's Ferry about sunrise next morning.

He reported his mode of procedure and the strategy used to render his safety certain from the Indians who had dispersed and driven the army before them. He was interrogated into the number, and when he reported TWENTY, great indignation was manifested by some of the *brave* volunteers who had got into camp some hours before him, and reported the number at fifteen hundred to two thousand! But as he was well known to many of the volunteers and highly respected as a meek and lowly Christian gentleman, they stood by him and prevented any personal violence.

When the report of this fiasco came into Galena the next morning about 8 o'clock, on the 15th of May, our regiment was immediately called to arms, as great danger was apprehended by the citizens. The general supposition was that the Pottowattomies and Winnebagoes had joined Black Hawk, it being well known that his entire band, including women and children, that had gone up Rock river, did not exceed one thousand persons. Dwellings were vacated and most of the inhabitants repaired to the stockades for safety.

The news of Stillman's defeat "by 2,000 blood-thirsty Indian warriors" spread fast, far and wide, and the Governor of Illinois called for more volunteers; and when the news reached Washington, the Secretary of War ordered Gen. Scott, then at New York, to take a thousand soldiers and proceed to the seat of war and take command of the army.

This violation of a flag of truce, the wanton murder of its bearers, and the attack upon a mere remnant of Black Hawk's band when sueing for peace, precipitated a war that should have been avoided.

(In confirmation of the dastardly act of the volunteers in killing the bearer of a white flag, and by which the war was precipitated, we give the following letter of Mr. Elijah Kilbourn, one of the scouts connected with Stillman's command. Mr. K. is the man Black Hawk makes mention of in his narrative as having been taken captive during our last war with Great Britain, and by him adopted into the Sac tribe; and again taken prisoner by three of his braves at the battle of Sycamore creek.)

Kilbourn's Narrative

A Reminiscence of Black Hawk

(From the Soldier's Cabinet)

MUCH HAS BEEN SAID BOTH for and against the Indian character; but we doubt whether greater or nobler qualities have ever been exhibited in the conduct of civilized rulers or commanders than are shown in the incidents we are about to relate concerning Black Hawk, whose deeds upon the northwestern frontier will render his name illustrious while history exists.

Elijah Kilbourn, the subject of the great chieftain's kindness, and to whom we are indebted for the present sketch, was a native of Pennsylvania. Just before the outbreak of the late war with Great Britain, he left the place of his birth to join the stirring scenes of adventure on the borders; and although now an old man, he still remembers, and loves to recount, the deed, and perils of his younger days, and especially those we are about to record.

"We had been," commenced Kilbourn, in whose own language the story shall be given, "scouting through the country that lay about Fort Stephenson, when early one morning one of our number came in with the intelligence that the Fort was besieged by a combined force of British and Indians. We were very soon after in our saddles, bearing down with all speed in that direction for the express purpose of joining in the fight—but on arriving, we found that the enemy had been signally repulsed by the brave little garrison under the command of Major Crogan. Our disappointment at learning this was, however, in a measure lessened, when we learned that Black Hawk, the leader of the savages, had, soon after the termination of the battle, gone with some twenty of his warriors back to his village on Rock river, whither we instantly determined to follow him.

"At sunrise the next morning we were on his trail, and followed it with great care to the banks of a stream. Here we ascertained that the savages had separated into nearly equal parties—the one keeping straight down the banks of the stream, while the other had crossed to the other side and continued on toward Rock river. A council was now held, in which the oldest members of our party gave it as their opinion that Black Hawk had changed his intention of going to his village, and had, with the greater part of his followers, pursued his way down the stream, while the rest had been sent by him for some purpose to the town. In this opinion all coincided; but still our leader, who was a very shrewd man, had some doubts on his mind concerning the movements of the chief, and therefore, to make everything sure, he detailed four of us to follow the trail across the stream, while he with the rest, some seven or eight in number, immediately took the one down the bank.

"We soon after found ourselves alone and in the vicinity of Indian settlements, and we were therefore obliged to move with the utmost caution, which had the effect of rendering our progress extremely slow. During the course of the following morning we came across a great many different trails and by these we were so perplexed that we resolved to return to the main body; but from the signs we had already seen we knew that such a step would be attended with the greatest risk, and so it was at last decided that it would be far more safe for all hands to separate, and each man look out for himself. This resolve was no sooner made than it was put into execution, and a few minutes later found me alone in the great wilderness. I had often been so before, but never before had I been placed in a situation as dangerous as the present one, for now on all sides I was surrounded by foes, who would rejoice in the shedding of my blood. But still I was not gong to give up easily, and looking well to my weapons and redoubling my caution, I struck off at an angle from the course I had first chosen, why I hardly knew.

"I encountered nothing very formidable till some two hours before sunset, when, just as I emerged from a tangled thicket, I perceived an Indian on his knees at a clear, sparkling spring, from which he was slaking his thirst. Instinctively I placed my rifle to my shoulder, drew a bead upon the savage and pulled the trigger. Imagine, if you can, my feelings as the flint came down and was shivered to pieces while the priming remained unignited.

"The next moment the savage was up on his feet, his piece levelled directly at me and his finger pressing the trigger. There was no escape; I had left my horse in the woods sometime before. The thicket behind me was too dense to permit me to enter it again quickly, and there was no tree within reach of sufficient size to protect me from the aim of my foe, who, now finding me at his mercy, advanced, his gun still in its threatening rest, and ordered me to surrender. Resistance and escape were alike out of the question, and I accordingly delivered myself up his prisoner, hoping by some means or other to escape at some future period. He now told me, in good English, to proceed in a certain direction. I obeyed him, and had not gone a stone's throw before, just as I turned a thick clump of trees, I came suddenly upon an Indian camp, the one to which my captor undoubtedly belonged.

"As we came up all the savages, some six or eight in number, rose quickly and appeared much surprised at my appearing thus suddenly amongst their number; but they offered me no harm, and they behaved with most marked respect to my captor, whom, upon a close inspection, I recognized to be Black Hawk himself.

"'The White mole digs deep, but Makataimeshekiakiak (Black Hawk) flies high and can see far off,' said the chieftain is a deep, gutteral tone, addressing me.

"He then related to his followers the occasion of my capture, and as he did so they glared on me fiercely and handled their weapons in a threatening manner, but at the conclusion of his remarks they appeared better pleased, although I was the recipient of many a passing frown. He now informed me that he had told his young men that they were to consider me a brother, as he was going to adopt me into the tribe.

"This was to me but little better than death itself, but there was no alternative and so I was obliged to submit, with the hope of making my escape at some future time. The annunciation of Black Hawk, moreover, caused me great astonishment, and after pondering the matter I was finally forced to set down as its cause one of those unaccountable whims to which the savage temperment is often subject.

"The next morning my captors forced me to go with them to their village on Rock river, where, after going through a tedious ceremony, I was dressed and painted, and thus turned from a white man into an Indian.

"For nearly three years ensuing it was my constant study to give my adopted brothers the slip, but during the whole of that time I was so carefully watched and guarded that I never found an opportunity to escape.

"However, it is a long lane that has no turning, and so it proves in my case. Pretending to be well satisfied with my new mode of life, I at last gained upon the confidence of the savages, and one day when their vigilance was considerably relaxed, I made my escape and returned in safety to my friends, who had mourned for me as dead.

"Many years after this I was a participant in the battle at Sycamore

Creek, which, as you know, is a tributary of Rock river. I was employed by the government as a scout, in which capacity it was acknowledged that I had no superior; but I felt no pride in hearing myself praised, for I knew I was working against Black Hawk, who, although he was an Indian, had once spared my life, and I was one never to forget a kindness. And besides this I had taken a great liking to him, for there was something noble and generous in his nature. However, my first duty was to my country, and I did my duty at all hazards.

"Now you must know that Black Hawk, after moving west of the Mississippi, had recrossed, contrary to his agreement, not, however, from any hostile motive, but to raise a crop of corn and beans with the Pottowattomies and Winnebagoes, of which his own people stood in the utmost need. With this intention he had gone some distance up Rock river, when an express from General Atkinson ordered him peremptorily to return. This order the old chief refused to obey, saying that the General had no right to issue it. A second express from Atkinson threatened Black Hawk that if he did not return peaceably, force would be resorted to. The aged warrior became incensed at this and utterly refused to obey the mandate, but at the same time sent word to the General that he would not be the first one to commence hostilities.

"The movement of the renowned warrior was immediately trumpeted abroad as an invasion of the State, and with more rashness thin wisdom, Governor Reynolds ordered the Illinois militia to take the field, and these were joined by the regulars, under General Atkinson, at Rock Island. Major Stillman, having under his command two hundred and seventy-five mounted men, the chief part of whom were volunteers, while a few like myself were regular scouts, obtained leave of General Whitesides, then lying at Dixon's Ferry, to go on a scouting expedition.

"I knew well what would follow; but still, as I was under orders, I was obliged to obey, and together with the rest proceeded some thirty miles up Rock river to where Sycamore creek empties into it. This brought us to within six or eight miles of the camp of Black Hawk, who, on that day—May 14th-was engaged in preparing a dog feast for the purpose of fitly celebrating a contemplated visit of some Pottawattomie chiefs.

"Soon after preparing to camp we saw three Indians approach us bearing a white flag; and these, upon coming up, were made prisoners. A second deputation of five were pursued by some twenty of our mounted militia, and two of them killed, while the other three escaped. One of the party that bore the white flag was, out of the most cowardly vindictiveness, shot down while standing a prisoner in camp. The whole detachment, after these atrocities, now bore down upon the camp of Black Hawk, whose braves, with the exception of some forty or fifty, were away at a distance.

"As we rode up, a galling and destructive fire was poured in upon us by the savages, who, after discharging their guns, sprung from their coverts on either side, with their usual horrible yells, and continued the attack with their tomahawks and knives. My comrades fell around me like leaves; and happening to cast my eyes behind me, I beheld the whole detachment of militia flying from the field. Some four or five of us were left unsupported in the very midst of the foe, who, renewing their yells, rushed down upon us in a body. Gideon Munson and myself were taken prisoners, while others were instantly tomahawked and scalped. Munson, during the afternoon, seeing, as he supposed, a good opportunity to escape, recklessly attempted to do so, but was immediately shot down by his captor. And I now began to wish that they would serve me in the same manner, for I knew that if recognized by the savages, I should be put to death by the most horrible tortures. Nothing occurred, however, to give me any real uneasiness upon this point till the following morning, when Black Hawk, passing by me, turned and eyed me keenly for a moment or so. Then, stepping close to me, he said in a low tone: *'Does the mole think that Black Hawk forgets?'*

"Stepping away with a dignified air, he now left me, as you may well suppose, bordering in despair, for I knew too well the Indian character to imagine for a single instant that my life would be spared under the circumstances. I had been adopted into the tribe by Black Hawk, had lived nearly three years among them, and by escaping had incurred their displeasure, which could only be appeased with my blood. Added to this, I was now taken prisoner at the very time that the passions of the savages were most highly wrought upon by the mean and cowardly conduct of the whites. I therefore gave up all hope, and doggedly determined to meet stoically my fate.

"Although the Indians passed and repassed me many times during the day, often bestowing on me a buffet or a kick, yet not one of them seemed to remember me as having formerly been one of the tribe. At times this infused me with a faint hope, which was always immediately after extinguished, as I recalled to mind my recognition by Black Hawk himself.

"Some two hours before sunset Black Hawk again came to where I was bound, and having loosened the cords with which I was fastened to a tree, my arms still remaining confined, bade me follow him. I immediately obeyed him, not knowing what was to be my doom, though I expected none other than death by torture. In silence we left the encampment, not one of the savages interfering with us or offering me the slightest harm or indignity. For nearly an hour we strode on through the gloomy forest, now and then starting from its retreat some wild animal that fled upon our approach. Arriving at a bend of the river my guide halted, and turning toward the sun, which was rapidly setting, he said, after a short pause:

"'I am going to send you back to your chief, though I ought to kill you for running away a long time ago, after I had adopted you as a son—but Black Hawk can forgive as well as fight. When you return to your chief I want you to tell him all my words. Tell him that Black Hawk's eyes have looked upon many sum, but they shall not see many more; and that his back is no longer straight, as in his youth, but is beginning to bend with age. The Great Spirit has whispered among the tree tops in the morning and evening and says that Black Hawk's days are few, and that he is wanted in the spirit land. He is half dead, his arm shakes and is no longer strong, and his feet are slow on the war path. Tell him all this, and tell him, too,' continued the untutored hero of the forest, with trembling emotion and marked emphasis, 'that Black Hawk would have been a friend to the whites, but they would not let him, and that the hatchet was dug up by themselves and not by the Indians. Tell your chief that Black Hawk meant no harm to the pale faces when he came across the Mississippi, but came peaceably to raise corn for his starving women and children, and that even then he would have gone back, but when he sent his white flag the braves who carried it were treated like squaws and one of them inhumanly shot. Tell him too,' he concluded with terrible force, while his eyes fairly flashed fire, 'that Black Hawk will have revenge, and that he will never stop until the Great Spirit shall say to him, 'come away.'

"Thus saying he loosened the cord that bound my arms, and after giving me particular directions as to the best course to pursue to my own camp, bade me farewell and struck off into the trackless forest, to commence that final struggle which was decided against the Indians.

"After the war was over, and the renowned Black Hawk had been taken prisoner, he was sent to Washington and the largest cities of the seaboard, that he might be convinced how utterly useless it was for him to contend against fate. It was enough, and the terrible warrior returned to the seclusion of his wilderness home, while the scepter of his chieftainship was given to the celebrated Keokuk.

"On the occasion of the ceremony by which Black Hawk was shorn of his power, and which took place on Rock Island, in the Mississippi, I shook the hand of the great chief, who appeared highly pleased to meet me once more; and upon parting with me he said with mournful dignity, as he cast above him a glance of seeming regret: 'My children think I am too old to lead them anymore!'

"This was the last time I ever saw him; and the next I learned of him was that he had left his old hunting grounds forever, and his spirit had gone to that bar where the balance will be rightly adjusted between the child of the forest and his pale face brethren."

Although the Winnebagoes and the Pottowattomies had resolved to take no part in the war, a few young men from each of these tribes, being emboldened by Black Hawk's victory in the engagement with Stillman's regiment, concluded to join him. As the party moved up the river, war parties were sent out, in one of which the Winnebagoes joined, whilst the Pottowattomies, some twenty-five or thirty, went alone on the war path into a settlement that had been made on Indian creek, not far from its entrance into Fox river, and killed fifteen men, women and children, and took two young ladies prisoners, the Misses Hall, whom two young Sacs, who had just rode up, took upon their horses and carried them to a Winnebago camp, with a request that they be delivered to the whites. They were returned soon after, and to the writer said they had been well treated by the Winnebagoes.

On the 19th of Jane a message came into Galena from Kellogg's Grove, with a report that a party of Indians had been seen in that neighborhood and that they had stolens some horses. Captain James Stephenson, with twelve picked men from his company, started immediately in pursuit of the Indians. On seeing him approach they took to the brush, when the Captain and his men dismounted. Leaving one to hold the horses, the balance entered the thicket, and two of them were killed at the first fire of the Indians, while three of the enemy were laid prostrate. For the purpose of re-loading, Capt. Stephenson ordered a retreat, which was a bad move, as it gave the Indians time to re-load and seek trees for safety. Capt. Stephenson* and party again advanced, both parties firing simultaneously, each losing a man, when an Indian who had been secreted behind a tree rushed forward with his knife, but was suddenly checked by one of the soldiers running his bayonet through him. While in this position he seized the bayonet with both hands and had almost succeeded in pushing it out, when another soldier rushed forward, and with one stroke of his knife almost severed the head from his body. In this engagement Capt. S. lost three of the best men of his company and the Indians five, just one-half of their number.

On the return of Capt. Stephenson and party the news of his loss of three men, who were well known and highly respected, soon spread over town and caused much sorrow among their many friends. After learning the mode of attack, military men generally criticized it severely.

Battle of Pecatonica

ON THE 14TH OF JUNE, a mall scouting party of Sacs killed five men at the Spafford farm, and on reception of the news next day, Gen. Atkinson ordered Col. Henry Dodge to take command of Posey's brigade, then stationed near Fort Hamilton, and while on his way from Fort Union, where his regiment was in camp, to visit the brigade, he heard the sharp crack of a rifle, and instantly looking in the direction of the sound, saw a man fall from his horse, who had been shot by Indians nearby. Instead of going forward as he set out to do, he hastily returned to his command, mustered a portion of his cavalry and went in pursuit of the Indians, and soon got on the trail of twenty-five warriors, who had commenced their retreat soon after shooting, and espying him, hastened back to the front. The Indians crossed and recrossed the Pecatonica river several times, being closely pushed by Col. Dodge and his men, and finding escape hopeless, made a stand. The colonel immediately dismounted his men and picked his way cautiously, with the intention of firing and then charging upon them. But the Indians, being on the lookout, watched their opportunity and got the first fire, by which a brave soldier named Apple was killed, and another by the

---

* Capt. Stephenson was held in high estimation as a brave and accomplished gentleman, and at the organization of Rock Island county the county commissioners honored his name by calling the county seat Stephenson, which name it retained until after his death, when that of Rock Island was adopted.

name of Jenkins was wounded. The fight continued vigorously until the last Indian was killed, several of them having been shot while trying to escape by swimming. At the commencement of the fight, the forces on each side were nearly equal, but the Indians, in swimming the river, had got their powder wet, and although they made desperate efforts to close in on our men with knives, they were shot down in their endeavors.

Col. Dodge, in speaking of this engagement, at Galena, after the close of the war, said he was amazed at the desperation displayed by a big, burly brave, who came towards him with gun at his shoulder and halted quickly when only a few paces from him, drew the trigger, and was sorely disappointed in his gun not going off. Quick as thought the colonel brought his rifle in position, pulled the trigger, but, owing to the dampness of the powder, it failed to go off. In the meantime the brave was coming towards him, knife in hand and desperation in his eye, and when only a few feet from him the colonel shot him down with his revolver. At the same time one of his brave boys, by the name of Beach, was engaged in a desperate encounter with the last remaining savage, in which both used knives; the Indian was killed and Beach very badly wounded.

Thus ended one of the most sanguinary engagements of the war.

Fight at Apple River Fort

CAPT. A.W. SNYDER'S COMPANY, OF Col. Henry's Regiment, was detailed to guard the country between Galena and Fox and Rock rivers, and was surprised on the night of the 17th of June, while encamped in the vicinity of Burr Oak Grove. His sentinels, while on duty, were fired upon by Indians, who did not deem it prudent to continue the attack, but immediately fled. As soon as it was light enough next morning to follow their trail, Capt. Snyder started with his company, but on reaching their camp, found that they had fled on his approach. He redoubled his speed and continued on their trail until he overtook them. Finding that there was no escape, the Indians got into a deep gully for protection, but were soon surrounded, when Capt. Snyder ordered his men to charge upon them. The Indians fired as they approached and mortally wounded one of his men, Mr. William B. Mekemson, a brave volunteer from St. Clair county, (whose father's family afterwards settled in this, Henderson county, all of whom, except one brother, Andrew, a highly respected Christian gentleman, have, long since, gone to meet their kinsman in another world.) Mr. M. being unable to ride, a rude litter was made and men detailed to carry him back to camp, at Kellogg's Grove. The company had not proceeded far before they were attacked by about seventy-five Indians, and two men, Scott and McDaniel, killed, and a Mr. Cornelius wounded. The company was soon formed into line by the aid of Gen. Whiteside, who was then acting merely as a private, and using the precaution of Indians, each man got behind a tree, and the battle waxed furiously for sometime without any serious results, until the Indian commander was seen to fall, from the well directed aim of Gen. Whiteside's rifle. Having now no leader the Indians ingloriously fled, but for some reason were not pursued. Our reporter, however, said that most of the company refused, for the reason that the second term of their enlistment had expired, and they were anxious to be mustered out of service, although the officers were eager to pursue.

The company then commenced their march to camp, and on approaching the litter on which Mekemson lay, found that the Indians had cut off his head and rolled it down the hill. Soon after, Major Riley, with a small force of regulars, came up, and after consultation with Capt. Snyder, it was deemed best not to follow the retreating Indians, as their route probably led to the main army of Black Hawk.

Apple River Fort

ON THE 23D OF JUNE scouts came into Galena, and reported at headquarters that a large body of Indians had been seen about thirty miles distant, but not being on the march, they were not able to conjecture to what point they were going. Col. Strode immediately made all necessary preparations to receive them, should Galena be the point of attack, and dispatched an express early next morning for Dixon's Ferry. On their arrival at Apple River Fort they halted for a short time, and then proceeded on their journey, and while yet in sight, at the crack of a gun the foremost man was seen to fall from his horse and two or three Indians rushed upon him with hatchets raised ready to strike, while his comrades galloped up, and with guns pointed towards the Indians kept them at bay until the wounded man reached the Fort. But had the Indians known these guns were *not loaded,* (as afterwards reported) they could have dispatched all three of them with their tomahawks.

In a very short time after hearing the crack of the gun a large body of Indians surrounded the fort, yelling and shooting, when the inmates, under command of Capt. Stone, prepared for defence, every port hole being manned by sharp-shooters. One man, Mr. George Herclurode, was shot through a port hole and instantly killed, and Mr. James Nutting wounded in the same way, but not seriously; which was the only loss sustained during the engagement of more than one hour's duration. A number of Indians were wounded and carried off the field. Capt. Stone had only twenty-five men, with a large number of women and children in the fort, but had providentially received a quantity of lead and provisions from Galena only an hour before the attack, and as he was short of bullets, the ladies of the fort busied themselves in melting lead and running balls as long as the battle lasted. Black Hawk, finding the fort impregnable from assault without firing it—an act that he well knew would, in a very short time, have brought a large body of troops on his path—concluded that it would be better to return and carry with them all the flour they could, killed a number of cattle and took choice pieces of beef, and all the homes that were in the stable. One of the expressmen, not deeming the fort a place of safety, hurried back to Galena, but getting lost on the way did not get in until early next morning. On hearing the news, Col. Strode took one hundred picked men, well mounted, and went to the relief of the fort, and was much gratified to find that its noble defenders had put to flight about one hundred and fifty Indians who had been under the command of Black Hawk himself.

Kellogg's Grove Fort

AFTER LEAVING APPLE RIVER FORT, being well supplied with provisions, the Indians moved leisurely toward the fort at Kellogg's Grove, with the intention of taking it, as scouts had come in and reported that it was not very strongly garrisoned on the day previous to their arrival on the 23d of June. At this time the Illinois troops were rendez-voused at a place known as Fort Wilbourn on the Illinois river, at or near where now stands the city of LaSalle. What was then called the new levy, after Stillman's defeat, were assembled there, numbering about three thousand men, being formed into military organizations consisting of three brigades. The first brigade was commanded by Gen. Alexander Posey. The second by Gen. M. K. Alexander, and the third by Gen. James D. Henry. Major John Dement, of Vandalia, was elected to the command of a spy battalion composed of three companies. Gen. Atkinson, of the United States Regulars, commanding, while these organizations were progressing.

The Indians had made a raid on Bureau creek, situated between the Illinois and Rock rivers. John Dement had been chosen major by the members of three companies of Gen. Posey's brigade, which was a spy battalion. The Major's battalion being ready for duty when the news reached the fort of the attack upon the settles on Bureau creek, it was ordered to march at once to the scene of danger for protection of the settlers, and to discover and watch the movements of the Indians, if possible. The Major was ordered to scour the country through to Rock river, and then to report to Col. Zackary Taylor, who commanded a small force of United States troops at a small fortification at Dixon's Ferry on Rock river.

On the 22d of June, 1832, Major Dement reached Colonel Taylor's command, having performed the duties to which he was assigned by General Atkinson. On his arrival Colonel Taylor informed the Major that he had arrived at an opportune time, as he wished him to take his command, swim their horses across the river, and promptly occupy the country between his position and the Lead Mines at Galena, a distance of about sixty miles, with headquarters at Kellogg's Grove, thirty-seven miles in the direction of Galena and Apple River Fort. There had been stationed at the grove two companies of Regulars, commanded by Major Riley, and three companies of Volunteers that had abandoned this position the day before the arrival of Major Dement, and left the country without protection and entirely unguarded. These troops had been engaged in two or three skirmishes with the Indians, and according to the reports of the soldiers, had been worsted in each. Major Dement's command numbered one hundred and forty men, all told, not one of whom had ever seen any military experience, but they were men to be relied upon. They were citizen soldiers, brave and intelligent, equal to any emergency, and had no superiors in the service. This being an odd battalion, Major Dement was entitled to the staff of a Colonel. His staff was composed of Zadoc Casey, Paymaster;— Anderson, Colonel Hicks, and others. The Captains of the companies, and the staff officers, were leading citizens, who had, at short warning, left their several avocations to engage in defending the country against the attacks of the Indians.

Major Dement's Battle with the Indians

ON THE EVENING OF THE second day, after crossing Rock river, the Major's command marched to the stockade at Kellogg's Grove and encamped. In the morning, learning that Indian traces had been seen four or five miles from the grove, twenty-five volunteers were called for to go out and reconnoitre. This number was quickly filled, nearly everyone volunteering being an officer, and, as it afterward turned out, they were unfortunately accepted. These volunteers had not yet gotten out of sight of their camp, before three Indians were seen on their ponies between the fort and a small grove on the prairie, riding backward and forward. The reconnoitering party started after them in one, two and three order, according to the speed of their horses, while the Indians made straight for the small grove. Major Dement, who was watching the movements of the volunteers from his camp, and seeing the movements of the Indians, at once suspected a trap, mounted with a portion of his men, and went to their aid. His men that had first started were a mile out upon the prairie in pursuit of those few Indians. Being well mounted, the Major and his relief party soon overtook the hindermost of the little band, but several were too far in advance in their mad pursuit of the fleeing Indians for him to reach them in time. The fleeing Indians were making for a grove some three miles away, hotly pursued by the Major's men. In this grove, as the commander feared, a large number of the Indians were concealed. When within four or five hundred yards of this grove he halted and dismounted his men and formed them in line. Some six or seven of his men were still in advance following the Indians toward this grove. On nearing the grove, his men who were in advance, were received with a galling fire, which killed two and wounded a third. With hideous yells the Indians emerged from the grove and rapidly approached. They were all mounted, stripped to their waists and painted for battle. As they reached the bodies of the dead soldiers, a large number surrounded them, clubbing and stabbing their lifeless remains. A volley from the rifles of the whites killed two or three at this point, but by the time the last of the little band had reached the ridge upon which their comrades were drawn up in line, the Indians were close upon them and on both flanks. At this point three men who had been out of their camp hunting for their homes, came in sight and were massacred in sight of their friends. The main portion of the battalion had been ordered to hold themselves in readiness for any emergency, but hearing the yelling, instead of obeying the order, mounted in hot haste and started to the rescue of their companions. On discovering the force of the Indians, they retreated to the grove, and almost neck and neck with the Indians, sprang over their horses and occupied the Block House.

On the least exposed side of the Fort was a work bench; over this the Major threw the bridle rein of his horse, and most of the horses huddled around this as if conscious of their danger. The Indians swarmed around the Block House under cover; an ominous stillness pervaded the air, which was soon broken by the crack of the rifles of the white men. The best marksmen with the best guns were stationed at the port holes, and a lively fire was kept up by the little garrison. The Indians finding that they were making no impression, turned their attention to shooting the horses, twenty-five of which they succeeded in killing. After sharp firing for two hours they retreated, leaving nine of their men dead on the field. This was the first engagement in this war, in which the whites had held their position until reinforcements arrived, without retreating. If the main force had remained in the grove at this Block House after the volunteers went out, without making any demonstration when the Indians came charging up and still in the open prairie, they could have been easily repulsed. This was the Major's plan of action, but the men became excited by the firing, and having no commissioned officers to guide them, started without order to assist their exposed comrades in the open prairie, when they were flying for their lives to the block house.

That evening Gen. Posey came up with his brigade, and although the Indians were encamped a short distance away, he made no effort to attack them but contented himself with reporting the situation to Col. Z. Taylor at Dixon's Ferry. Gen. Whiteside had said to Major Dement before crossing Rock river, that he was going into the Indian rendezvous, where he could have an Indian for breakfast every morning, and he found it literally true.

It seems strange that Major Dement should have been ordered by Col. Taylor into the enemy's country, across Rock river, with so small a force of volunteers, while a large force of Regulars and Volunteers, commanded by regular United States officers, remained securely entrenched in the rear. It was Major Dement's opinion that there were more fighting men of Black Hawk's band of warriors in the engagement at Kellogg's Grove than ever afterwards made a stand during the war. It was easy for Gen. Posey to have moved up and attacked the Indians on his arrival at the Grove, and then have dealt them a fatal blow by forcing them to battle then, but he refused to do so, and the war was not terminated until the fight at Bad Axe some two months later, in which the Illinois troops did not engage. During this engagement at the Block House, four whites and eleven Indians were killed. The whites lost a large part of their horses—the Indians shooting them from the timber, while the poor animals were huddled about the Block House.

Although in command, Black Hawk remained in the Grove doing the engagement, looking on to see that his principal aid, whose voice was like a trumpet call, carried out his orders.

While reciting the incidents of this battle to the author, when writing his Autobiography, Black Hawk spoke in high praise of Major Dement as a commander, who had shown not only good military skill in coming to the rescue of his party, but in withdrawing his little party to the Fort. After Dement's engagement General Posey's brigade started for Fort Hamilton and remained there a short time. News of Dement's engagement and march of Posey's brigade having been received at Dixon's Ferry, where the two other brigades were stationed, Gen. Alexander, with the 2d brigade was ordered to cross Rock river and march to Plum river to intercept the Indians, as it was deemed probable that they would make for that point to cross the Mississippi. Gen. Atkinson, with regulars, and Gen. Fry with his brigade, remained at Dixon waiting for news of the route taken by the Indians. Next day Capt. Walker and three Pottowottamie Indians came into Dixon and reported seventy-five Pottowottamies ready to join the army now encamped at Sycamore creek, and they were afraid that Black Hawk and his army was not far off. For their protection, and to await the coming of the balance of the second brigade, Col. Fry, of Henry's brigade, was sent forward immediately. The next morning Gen. Henry's brigade moved forward with Gen. Atkinson at the head, intending to march up Rock river, to the Four Lakes, and camped at Stillwell's battle-ground the first night and joined Col. Fry and his Pottowottamie Indians on the 29th, and continued their march. On the 30th, when going into camp, they saw signs of Sac Indians, but the sentinels were undisturbed during the night. The next day they saw one Indian, but he was on the other side of Plum river. On the 2d of July, Major Ewing being in front, spied a fresh trail, and soon after came upon the fresh trail of Black Hawk's entire force, at a point near Keeshkanawy Lake. Scouts from the battalion came up to Black Hawk's encampment, from which they had apparently taken their departure a few days before. Here they found five white men's scalps which had been left hung up to dry. This battalion continued to march around the lake in detachments, one of which found where there had been another encampment, but on returning to camp and comparing notes they began to despair of finding the main body of Black Hawk's army in that region. On the 5th of July, Gen. Atkinson with his army took a rest. During the day some scouts brought in an old Indian nearly blind and half famished with hunger, whom the Indians had left in their flight. After eating, Gen. Atkinson questioned him closely as to the whereabouts of Black Hawk and his army, but was satisfied from his replies and helpless condition, that he did not know, but on taking up his line of march the near morning, Gen. Atkinson did not leave him as the Indians had done, alone and without any means of subsistence, but left him an abundance of food, and as we afterwards learned, the old man recruited and afterwards got back to his tribe.

On the evening of the 9th the army encamped at White Water, and the next morning Indians were seen on the other side of this stream which was not fordable, one of whom shot and wounded a regular. After breaking camp, Gen. Atkinson ordered a move up the river, and that night camped with his entire force—all having met at the same point. Gen. Dodge's corps had taken a Winnebago prisoner and brought him into camp for the purpose of finding out if he knew where Black Hawk's forces were. He said they were encamped on an island near Burnt Village. Col. William S. Hamilton, a brave and honored son of Alexander Hamilton, in command of a company of Menomonees, who had joined the main army the day before, with Captain Early and his command, after scouring the island thoroughly, reported there were no Indians on the island.

Governor Reynolds, who had been on the march up Rock River with his volunteers and the main army, together with Colonel Smith, Major Sidney Breese and Colonel A. P. Field, left the army and came into Galena on the 12th, from whom we obtained our information of the movements of the army. They were firmly of the opinion that the Indians had taken to the swamps, and gotten entirely out of reach of the army, and that no farther danger need be apprehended. Colonel Field, who is an eloquent speaker, at the solicitation of Colonel Strode, although nearly worn out with hard marches, made an able and soul-stirring speech to our regiment, and a large number of the inhabitants of Galena.

At this time the army was nearly out of provisions, and Fort Winnebago, about seventy-five miles distant, the nearest point at which they could replenish. General Atkinson then ordered General Posey with his brigade, to Fort Hamilton, General Henry's and Alexander's brigade and General Dodge's squadron to Fort Winnebago for provisions; and sent General Ewing and his regiment to Dixon with Colonel Dunn, who had been seriously wounded by one of his own sentinels, but who afterwards recovered. General Atkinson then built a fort near the camping ground, which was Fort Keeshkanong. General Alexander returned on the 15th with provisions to the fort, while Generals Dodge and Henry thought best to go with their commands to the head of Fox river, and while on the way stopped at a Winnebago village and had a talk with their head men, who assured them that Black Hawk was then at Cranberry Lake, a point higher up Rock river. After a consultation by the Generals, it was deemed best to send an express to General Atkinson at Fort Keeshkanong, to let him know of the information they had got, and their intention of moving on the enemy the next morning. Dr. Merryman, of Colonel Collins' regiment, and Major Woodbridge, Adjutant of General Dodge's corps, volunteered to go, and with Little Thunder, a Winnebago chief, as pilot, started out to perform this dangerous service, and after traveling a few miles, came on fresh Indian trails, which Little Thunder pronounced to have been made by Black Hawk's party, and fearing that they would be intercepted, insisted on returning to camp. Night was then approaching, and having no guide to lead them forward, they reluctantly followed Little Thunder back to camp. Orders were then given for an early move next morning, and at daylight the bugle sounded, and the army moved onwards. The trail was followed for two days, leading for Four Lakes. On the second day, July 21st, scouts from General Dodge's corps came in and reported Indians, and as a confirmation of the fact, Dr. A.K. Philleo exhibited a scalp that he had taken from the head of one that he had shot. Dr. Philleo was brave as the bravest, and whenever a scouting party started out to look for Indians (unless his services were required in camp), was always in the lead, and this being his first Indian, took his scalp, and sent it to the writer, with written instructions how to preserve it. To this end we handed over both to a deaf and dumb printer in the office, who boasted somewhat of his chemical knowledge, who spent considerable time for a number of days in following the Doctor's instructions. After the killing of this Indian, some of the scouts discovered fresh signs of more Indians, and after pursuing it for some miles, Dr. Philleo and his friend Journey, equally as brave, being in the lead, espied two more Indians, when each picked his man and fired, and both fell; one of them, although badly wounded, fired as he fell, and wounded one of the scouts. The Doctor's attention was now directed to his wounded companion, hence his second Indian was allowed to retain his scalp.

The scouts, finding that the trail was fresh, and the Indians were rapidly retreating, having strewed their trail with camp equipage, in order to facilitate their movements, sent an express back to camp, when the army hastily took up the line of march, with Dodge's corps and Ewing's Spy battalion in the front. By fast riding they soon came up with the Indians, whom they found already in line to receive them.

At Wisconsin Heights

ORDERS WERE AT ONCE GIVEN to dismount (leaving enough to hold the horses) and charge upon the Indians. They had scarcely time to form into line when they were met by the yelling Indians and a heavy volley from their guns.

Dodge and Ewing ordered a charge, and as they moved forward, returned the fire at close quarters, with deadly effect. The Indians then commenced a flank movement, and by securing a position in the high grass where they could in a measure conceal themselves, fought bravely, until Dodge and Ewing gave orders to charge upon them at the point of the bayonet. In this engagement Col. Jones had his horse shot from under him, and one man killed—but at the word *"charge,"* he went forward with his brave men, and all performed their duty nobly and fearlessly, and soon dislodged the Indians from their hiding place and forced them into a hasty retreat. It being then too late to pursue them, orders were given to camp on the battle-ground.

In this engagement Neapope had command, who was not only brave and fearless, but well skilled in strategy. Having become well acquainted with him after the war, he told the writer that he knew Gen. Dodge personally, and had met him on the field of battle, and considered him one of the bravest men he had ever met, although in this engagement all the officers showed great skill and bravery, and thus encouraged their men to acts of noble daring to a degree that he had never before witnessed in common—not regular—soldiers. He said in this engagement, the command had been entrusted to him of this small force—about two hundred—Indians, in order to give Black Hawk and the remainder of his party, time to cross the river. He reported his loss at twenty-eight (28) killed.

The newt morning a portion of the army was ordered forward to pursue the fleeing enemy, but on reaching the river, found that they had taken to the swamps, when it was deemed prudent to return to camp without attempting to follow them.

Here the army rested for one day, and made comfortable provisions to carry the wounded, after having consigned the remains of John Short, who had been killed the day before, to mother Earth, with the honors of war.

In the meantime, Gen. Atkinson arrived with his regulars and the brigades of Generals Posey and Alexander; and on the 28th of July, took up the line of march with Gen. Atkinson at the head. Their route led through a mountainous country for several days, as the Indiana seemed to have selected the most difficult route they could find in order to gain time, and reach the river in advance, and then secure the best possible positions to defend themselves.

Having learned from an old Indian that had been left behind, that the enemy was only a short distance ahead, Gen. Atkinson, on breaking camp at an early hour in the morning, gave orders for the march towards the river, with Gen. Dodge's squadron in front; Infantry next; Second brigade, under command of Gen. Alexander, next; Gen. Posey's brigade next, and Gen. Henry's in the rear.

After marching a few miles Gen. Dodge's scouts discovered the rear guard of the enemy, when an express was sent immediately to Gen. Atkinson, who ordered troops to proceed at double quick. In the meantime Gen. Dodge's command pushed forward and opened a heavy fire, from which many Indians were shot down while retreating toward the Mississippi, where their main body was stationed. Dodge's squadron being in the lead, were first to open upon the main army of the Indians, whilst Gen. Henry's brigade, that had been placed in the rear in the morning, came first to his aid. The battle waged furiously for more than two hours, and until the last visible Indian warrior was killed. The Indians had commenced crossing before the battle opened, and a number took to their canoes and made good their escape as the battle progressed. The number killed was estimated at something over one hundred, but the Indians afterward reported their loss at seventy-eight killed and forty-two wounded. Our loss was seventeen killed and about the same number wounded.

During the engagement several squaws were killed accidentally and a number wounded, including children, who were taken prisoners. Among the latter, Dr. Philleo reported a boy with one arm badly broken, who exhibited a greater degree of stoicism during the operation of amputation, than he had ever before witnessed. Being very hungry, they gave him a piece of bread to eat, which he ravenously masticated during the entire operation, apparently manifesting no pain whatever from the work of the surgeon.

Many of the Indians who got across the river in safety were afterwards killed by the Menomonees.

Steamboat Warrior's Fight

ON THE 2D OF AUGUST, 1832, the steamboat, Warrior, was lying at Prairie du Chien, and word having been received at the fort that Black Hawk's main army was then at, or near the river above, at a point designated for all to meet for the purpose of crossing the river, Lieut. Kingsbury took her in charge, and started up with one company, in order to intercept the Indians and prevent their crossing before the main army arrived, as he knew it was in close pursuit of them. The boat soon came in view of Indians on both sides of the river—Black Hawk and several lodges having already crossed over-when they were hailed by Lieut. Kingsbury. A white flag was hoisted by the Indians, and Black Hawk directed the Winnebago interpreter on board the Warrior, to say to his chief that he wanted him to send out his small boat so as he could go on board, a he desired to give himself up. The Winnebago, however, reported to the commander that they refused to bring their flag aboard. He then directed his interpreter to say that if they still refused he would open fire upon them. In reply, the interpreter said they still refused, when the Lieutenant directed his six-pounder to be fired among them, and also opened a musketry fire by his company. This was returned by the Indians, and the battle continued for sometime. Several Indians were killed at the first fire, after which the remainder sought protection behind trees, stumps, etc. It was then getting late in the afternoon, and as the boat was nearly out of wood they dropped down to the fort to replenish, and started back again the next morning. On reaching an island some miles above their battle-ground of the day before, they commenced to rake it with their six-pounder, supposing the Indians had taken shelter there, and the army considering it a salute, Gen. Atkinson returned it. Soon after the boat landed and took on board Gen. Atkinson and the regulars and then returned to Prairie du Chien. The Illinois volunteers were ordered to Dixon, at which place they were discharged, while the troops of the lead mines were mustered out at Galena. After the boat started down the evening before, Black Hawk and a few of his people left for the lodge of a Winnebago friend, and gave himself up. Thus ended a bloody war which had been forced upon Black Hawk by Stillman's troops violating a flag of truce, which was contrary to the rules of war of all civilized nations, and one that had always been respected by the Indians. And thus, by the treachery or ignorance of the Winnebago interpreter on board of the Warrior, it was bought to a close in the same ignoble way it commenced—disregarding a flag of truce—and by which Black Hawk lost more than half of his army. But in justice to Lieut. Kingsbury, who commanded the troops on the Warrior, and to his credit it must be said, that Black Hawk's flag would have been respected if the Winnebago, who acted as his interpreter on the boat, had reported him correctly.

General Atkinson's Report

HEADQUARTERS FIRST ARTILLERY CORPS, NORTH-WESTERN ARMY, Prairie du Chiens, Aug. 25, 1832.

SIR

I have the honor to report to you that I crossed the Ouisconsin on the 27th and 28th ultimo, with a select body of troops, consisting of the regulars under Colonel Taylor, four hundred in number, part of Henry's, Posey's and Alexander's brigades, amounting in all to 1,300 men, and immediately fell upon the trail of the enemy, and pursued it by a forced march, through a mountainous and difficult country, till the morning of the 2d inst., when we came up with his main body on the left bank of the Mississippi, nearly opposite the mouth of the Ioway, which we attacked, defeated and dispensed, with a loss on his part of about a hundred and fifty men killed, thirty men, women and children taken prisoners—the precise number could not be ascertained, as the greater potion was slain after being forced into the river. Our loss in killed and wounded, which is stated below, is very small in comparison with the enemy, which may be attributed to the enemy's being forced from his position by a rapid charge the commencement, and throughout the engagement the remnant of the enemy, cut up and disheartened, crossed to the opposite side of the river, and had fled into the interior, with a view, it is supposed, of joining Keokuk and Wapello's bands of Sacs and Foxes.

The horses of the volunteer troops being exhausted by long marches, and the regular troops without shoes, it was not thought advisable to continue the pursuit; indeed, a stop to the further effusion of blood seemed to be called for, till it might be ascertained if the enemy would surrender.

It is ascertained from our prisoners that the enemy lost in the battle of the Ouisconsin sixty-eight killed and a very large number wounded; his whole loss does not fall short of three hundred. After the battle on the Ouisconsin, those of the enemy's women and children, and some who were dismounted, attempted to make their escape by descending that river, but judicious measures being taken by Captain Loomis and Lieutenant Street, Indian Agent, thirty-two women and children and four men have been captured, and some fifteen men killed by the detachment under Lieutenant Ritner.

The day after the battle on the river, I fell down with the regular troops to this place by water, and the wounded men will join us today. It is now my purpose to direct, Keokuk to demand a surrender of the remaining principal men of the hostile party, which, from the large number of women and children we hold prisoners, I have every reason to believe will be compiled with. Should it not, they should be pursued and subdued, a step Major-General Scott will take upon his arrival.

I cannot speak too highly of the brave conduct of the regular and volunteer forces engaged in the last battle, and the fatiguing march that preceded it, and as soon as the reports of officers of the brigades and corps are handed in, they shall be submitted with further remarks:

5 killed, 6 wounded, 6th inft.

2 wounded, 5th inft.

1 Captain, 5 privates, Dodge's Bat., mounted.

1 Lieutenant, 6 privates, Henry's Bat.

1 private wounded, Alexander's.

1 private wounded Posey's.

I have the great honor to be, with great respect,

Your obedient servant,

H. ATKINSON,

Brevet Brig. Gen. U.S.A.

Maj. Gen. Macomb, Com. in Chief,

Washington

Appendix

At Yellow Banks

Among the many hundreds of troops that came to Yellow Bank—Oquawka—on their way to the sea of war, Major S. S. Phelps always spoke in high terms of their good discipline and gentlemanly conduct, except in one instance—that of a few persons in a company from McDonough county, who came over at a time when old chief Tama and his wife, who was noted for being the white man's friend, came over to get provisions for his little band. On seeing an Indian some of these soldiers, who had been using their canteens rather frequently, were eager to slay him, and not only threatened him but Major P. also, for harboring him. The officers seemed to have no control of these men—and just at a time when their threats were loudest of what they intended to do at the close of three minutes, Major P. and one of his clerks, Mr. Joseph Smart, were standing with their rifles cocked ready to make the first shot, a cry came from outside of the building, by one of the more peaceable soldiers, "Here comes another company, Capt. Peter Butler's, from Monmouth," when these would-be braves instantly retreated.

We are assured by one of Capt. B. 's company, Mr. James Ryason, that the foregoing is literally true, and that Major P. and Mr. Smart, afterwards, amid the threats of these same soldiers, escorted Tama and wife to the river bank to take their canoe to cross the river, and stood there with their guns, ready to protect the Indians until they got out of reach of gunshot—Smart threatening all the time to put a ball though the first man that attempted to shoot.

In order to appease the wrath of these soldiers and prevent some of them being killed, Capt. B. advised Maj. P. not to give Tama any provisions; but on the way down, Mr. Ryason says, Smart (who talked their language equal to a native born) told them to meet them at a certain point after night and they would be supplied; and that for the purpose of assisting Mr. Smart in taking supplies to Tama, he got leave of absence from the Captain until next morning.

Messrs. James Ryason and Gabriel Shot, both honorable and highly respected Christian gentlemen, are the only survivors of that company now residing in this county.

Tama's village, located on South Henderson, half a mile below the farm of Mr. John T. Cook, at Gladstone, was always noted as being the abode of friendly Indians. In the fall of 1829, some write men came in and made improvements on the land in the vicinity, and at the advice of Mr. Phelps, Tama crossed the river and made a new town at the mouth of Flint river on the Mississippi, and at the time of Black Hawk's raid into Illinois, it was the rendezvous of many young men who had been persuaded by Tama not to join Black Hawk. But when the news reached them of the indignities offered to their good old chief, they secretly determined to go upon the war path, and soon after four young Foxes started to cross the river and avenge the insult. On going up Henderson creek they espied Mr. William Martin while in the act of mowing, at a point near Little York, whom they shot and killed, and for fear of detection, immediately took to the brush. It being late when they got through the woods, they made a fire and camped just at the edge of the prairie.

Sometime after the shooting, friends of Mr. Martin discovered his lifeless body and after removing it to the home, started on the trail of his murderers, and followed it some distance through the underbrush, but wisely concluded, as it was growing late, to return and give the alarm. An express was sent to Capt. Butler during the night, who started out with his company early in the morning, and on emerging into the prairie discovered the camp fire of the Indians, add followed their trail to a slough in the Mississippi two miles below Keithsburgh. Here the Indians embarked in their canoes and were probably on the other side of the river by this time. A demand was immediately made upon Keokuk for the murderers, as they belonged to his band of Foxes, who surrendered two men to the commanding officer at Rock Island.

These Indians soon afterwards made their escape, and before the time fixed for their trial, Keokuk delivered four young men to Maj. Phelps, then sheriff of Warren county, to be tried for the offence. Maj. P. and his deputy, Mr. James Ryason, took them to Monmouth jail, where the following proceedings were had before the Circuit Court (for a copy of which we are indebted to George C. Rankin, Esq., now Circuit Clerk):

Warren County Circuit Court

WILLIAM MARTIN WAS SHOT AND scalped by two Indians, near Little York, Warren county, August 9th, 1832. In their report at the October term of the Warren Circuit Court, the Grand jurors say:

"Six or seven Indians of Keokuk's band of Sac and Fox Indians who were not included in the war path under Black Hawk and other chiefs of the Sac and Fox, nation, came over from the western bank of the Mississippi river to the inhabited parts of Warren county, in said State, and unlawfully and feloniously murdered the said William Martin in the most barbarous manner. That the names of the said Indians are unknown to the Grand Jury. That two of the said Indians have been heretofore given up by the chiefs of said Indians, that they were confined in the Fort at Rock Island for sometime but have made their escape, and are now at large in their own country. That the Grand jury cannot now find an indictment because the names of the said Indiana are unknown to said jury. But they recommend that the Governor of the State be furnished with a copy of this presentment, and that he be desired to request of the President of the United States that the whole of the said Indians concerned in the said murder may be demanded of the said Sac and Fox nation that they may be indicted and punished for murder under the authority of the laws of this State."

In compliance with the demand of the President, the chiefs surrendered four Indians, namely, with their Interpretations;

Sa-sa-pi-ma (he that troubleth).
Ka-ke-mo (he that speaks with something in his mouth).
I-o-nah (stay here).
Wa-pa-sha-kon (the white string).

Concerning which, the Grand jury at the June term 1833 say:
"From an examination made by this Grand Jury they we now able to state that the four Indians lately surrendered by the chiefs at the request of the President of the United States, are not the real murderers of Martin. The chiefs represent that at the time the demand was made the real offenders had escaped from the territory and power of their nation. That the prisoners now in custody volunteered themselves to be surrendered in place of those who escaped, and that from custom amongst Indians, they supposed this would be a sufficient compliance with the requisition of the President. The Grand jury will not positively say that the chiefs have prevaricated, but they do say that the demand already made has been eluded."

By a writ of habeas corpus, the four Indians above named were brought before the judge, presiding, Hon. Richard M. Young, June 14th, 1833, and released.

Indictment was returned against the real murderers, Shash-quo-washi, Muck-que-che-qua, Muck-qua-pal-ashah, and Was-a-wau-a-quot, who, "not having the fear of God before their eyes, but being moved and seduced by the instigations of the devil," killed Wm. Martin. The indictment was drawn by Thomas Ford, States Attorney, and recites that William Martin was shot a little below the shoulder blade. Among the witnesses named were Keokuk and Stabbing Chief. The guilty parties were never arrested, and a *nolle prosequi* was entered at the October term at court, 1835.

Gen. Scott Arrives at Chicago

GEN. SCOTT, WITH A FULL regiment of regulars, came up the lake and landed at Chicago about the 10th of July—the cholera in the meantime having broken out among his troops, from which several had died. While encamped at that point, it continued its virulence to such an extent, and in a number of cases fatally, that he deemed it best to much out on the high land, and soon after continued his journey, by slow marches, to Rock Island. On reaching Rock river, where Milan is now situated, the cholera had disappeared, and he went into camp with his entire regiment. The clear water of this beautiful stream was a Godsend to the many tired men, for the ablution of their bodies and the cleansing of their apparel, tents, etc., and seemed to have a general invigorating effect upon the entire regiment.

Gen. Scott then went over to Rock Island with two companies to garrison Fort Armstrong, and there learned the situation of affairs in the army, and the great reduction made in the ranks of Black Hawk's band of Indians, so that a final close of the war was daily expected.

A few days after their arrival at Fort Armstrong, symptoms of cholera again appeared among the troops of the company, and the physician in charge tried every known remedy to check it, but failed in every instance, and after running its course, which was usually about twenty-four hours, the patient died. During the first three or four days of its ravages, about one-half of that company had been consigned to their last resting place in the soldiers' cemetery.

Being on a visit to Rock Island at the time the cholera was raging, the writer, at the request of Col. Wm. Berry, (who had also come down from Galena to pay his respects to Gen. Scott,) accompanied him to the Fort and introduced him to the General. It was a very warm, but beautiful Sabbath, when we were admitted to the General's quarters, about 10 o'clock in the morning, and after the introduction of our friend and the usual salutations of the day, the General, after expressing his doubts of the propriety of admitting us into the Fort, forcibly and touchingly detailed the ravages that the cholera was making in his ranks. Medicine, in the hands of a skillful physician, seemed to have no effect to stay its progress, and he was just on the eve of trying a different remedy as we came in, and if we would join him in a glass of brandy and water, he would proceed at once to put it into execution. He said he was satisfied that brandy was a good antidote to cholera, and by its use many of his soldiers were still well.

The General's Remedy

THE GENERAL PULLED OFF HIS coat, rolled up his sleeves, and directed an orderly to tear off strips of red flannel, fill a bucket with brandy and carry them to the hospital. On arriving at the bedside of a patient he directed him to be stripped, and then with flannel soaked in brandy he rubbed his chest thoroughly, in order to bring on a reaction, in the meantime administering a little brandy with a spoon. In the course of half an hour he returned and reported progress. He said he left his patient free from pain, and directed a small portion of the brandy to be given occasionally.

The well soldiers, seeing that their General was not afraid of cholera, nor too proud to act as nurse to a sick soldier, took courage and insisted on his retiring, so that they could fill his place. Seeing that new life had been infused among the well soldiers, and a gleam of hope seeming to inspire the sick, he gave directions for them to continue, as he had commenced, and then retired.

On returning to his quarters he washed his hands, rolled down his sleeves, put on his uniform, and then invited us to take a little brandy. After listening to his mode of treatment, we casually remarked that it looked feasible, but at the same time reprehensible in the General of the army exposing himself in the performance of a duty that could be done as well by a common soldier. He gave us a look, and kept his eyes upon us as his giant form raised up, and, with a sweep of his sword arm, said in majestic tones: "Sir, it is the duty of a General to take care of his army; should he fall another can take his place; but, without an army his occupation is gone!"

The General's treatment was continued right along, and the result was that many of those attacked got well.

Soon after the close of the war, which terminated with the battle of Bad Axe, on the second day of August, 1832, he came to Galena, and, in conference with Governor John Reynolds, ordered the chiefs head men and warriors of the Winnebago Nation to meet them at Fort Armstrong, Rock Island, on the 15th day of September, 1832, for the purpose of holding a treaty.

At the time fixed by the Commissioners they were met by the chiefs, head men and warriors of the Winnebago Nation, with whom a treaty was made and concluded, by which the Winnebagoes ceded to the United States all the lands claimed by them lying to the south and east of Wisconsin river and the Fox river of Green Bay. The consideration of this cession on the part of the United States, to be a grant to the Winnebago Nation of a tract on the west side of the Mississippi river known as the neutral ground and annual annuities for twenty-seven years of $10,000 in specie and a further sum, not to exceed $3,000 annually, for the purposes of maintaining a farm and a school for the education of Winnebago children during the same period of twenty-seven years.

Treaty with Sacs and Foxes

After concluding the treaty with the Winnebagoes, and for the purpose of making a lasting peace with the Sacs and Foxes, these Commissioners held a treaty at the same place, and a week later, on the 21st day of September, with chiefs, head men and warriors of that confederate tribe. The Commissioners demanded, partly as indemnity for expenses incurred in the late war with Black Hawk's band and to secure future tranquility, a cession of a large portion of their country bordering on the frontiers. In consideration thereof the United States agree to pay to said confederate tribes annually, for thirty years, $20,000 in specie; also, to pay Messrs. Farnham and Davenport, Indian traders at Rock Island, the sum of $40,000, to be receipted for in full of all demands against said Indians. And, further, at the special request of said confederate tribes, the United States agree to grant, by letters patent, to their particular friend, Antoine LeClair, interpreter, one section of land opposite Rock Island and one section at the head of the rapids of the Mississippi river.

The City of Davenport, Iowa

This beautiful city now covers that "Section of land opposite Rock Island" that was donated by treaty to Antoine LeClair by the Sacs and Foxes, and also three or four more sections. At that time it was wholly uninhabited, the Foxes having removed their village from that point some three years before. As a town site it was regarded by strangers and travelers on steamboats as the most beautiful west of the Mississippi between St. Louis and St. Paul, and now, with its twenty-three thousand inhabitants, elegant residences, magnificent public buildings, fine churches, schoolhouses, extensive manufactories, and large business blocks, it Stands unrivalled as a beautiful city. It has ten miles of street railroads, affording easy access to all parts of the city. It has two daily papers, the *Gazette* and *Democrat*, (morning and evening) both ably conducted; and also a German daily and two weeklies. The river is spanned by an elegant bridge that was built at the cost of nearly a million dollars, which is used by the various railroads from East to West, and has a roadway for teams and pedestrians.

The City of Rock Island

Is LOCATED ON THE BANK of the river in Illinois, immediately opposite to Davenport, and is a large and flourishing city, with a population of about twelve thousand inhabitants. It has fine public buildings, elegant churches and residences, substantial business blocks, extensive manufactories and elegant water works. The city is lighted by electric lights, from high towers, that cast their refulgent rays over the entire city, which makes it the finest lighted city in the west. There are two daily papers, (morning and evening) *The Union* and *The Argus*, both enjoying the privilege of Press dispatches, and both issue weeklies. *The Rock Islander* is also published weekly, and all have the appearance of great prosperity. The professions are represented by men of fine ability, including some of wide reputation. The banking business is done principally by two National Banks, that have a deservedly high reputation, and are doing a large business. There are two first-class hotels—the Harper House and Rock Island House—and several of less pretentions. The city has large coal fields, in close proximity, with railroads running daily to and from the banks, by which the three cities are supplied.

The City of Moline

Is LOCATED TWO MILES UP the river from Rock Island, but connected with it by street railways. It has a population of over 8,000 inhabitants, and is extensively known from its many manufacturing establishments, which are supplied with water power from a dam across the river from the Island.

Fifty Years Ago

WHEN THE WRITER FIRST VISITED this most beautiful Island in the Mississippi river, then and now known as Rock Island, the ground on which the triplet cities of Davenport, Rock Island, and Moline now stands, was covered with prairie grass, and apparently a sterile waste as regards to the two former, whilst the latter was principally covered with timber. Now how changed! Then the site of Davenport was claimed to be the most beautiful on the west bank of the Mississippi, between St. Paul and St. Louis by Black Hawk and his confreres, who had traveled up and down the river in canoes, whilst his judgment was confirmed by thousands of passengers who viewed it from steamboats in after years.

The Triple Cities

ARE WIDELY KNOWN AS THE leading manufacturing cities of the great west, with railroads stretching out from ocean to ocean, and although the Mississippi makes a dividing line, they are united by a magnificent bridge, which makes their intercourse easier than over paved streets.

Rock Island, at that time, was excluded from settlement by the orders of Government, as it had been reserved, on the recommendation of Hon. Lewis Cass, whilst he was in the Senate and Cabinet, as a site for a United States Arsenal and Armory. Fort Armstrong was situated on the lower end of the Island, and was then in command of Col. William Davenport. The Sac and Fox agency (Maj. Davenport, agent,) stood on the bank of the river about half a mile above the Fort; next came the residence and office of Antoine Le Clair, United States Interpreter for the Sam and Foxes, and a little higher up, the residence, store-house and out buildings of Col. George Davenport, who had by an act of Congress, preempted a claim of two hundred acres of land running across the Island from bank to bank of the river. The Island is about two miles long, and being at the foot of the rapids has the best water power on the river, capable of running a much greater amount of machinery than is at present in operation. The entire Island is now owned and occupied by the Government, (the heirs of Col. Davenport having sold and deeded their interest), and is now used as an

Armory and Arsenal

WHICH ARE DESTINED TO BE in the near future, the most extensive works of the kind probably in the world. Indeed, army officers who have traveled extensively in the Old World, say they have never seen anything to compare with it, in elegant grounds, water power and buildings, and with such facilities for moving anything to and from the Arsenal. These works were commenced under the supervision of Gen. Rodman, the inventor of the Rodman gun, and since the death of the General, D. W. Flagler, Lieut. Col. of Ordinance, has been in command, and a more efficient and better qualified officer for the place could not have been found in the army.

There are already completed ten massive stone buildings, which are used for work shops, storage, etc., officers' quarters, both durable and comfortable, and many other buildings. The former residence of Col. George Davenport, (the House in which he as killed for money many years ago) built in 1831, of solid hewed timber, and afterwards weather-boarded, still stands unoccupied.

The Island is mostly covered with trees of different varieties, which are kept neatly trimmed, and is laid out like a park, with wide avenues extending its whole length, which makes the most elegant drives and shady walks for the thousands of visitors who flock to the Island to feast their eyes upon its magnificence.

The City of Keokuk, Iowa,

Is LOCATED AT THE FOOT of the Lower Rapids, 139 miles from Rock Island, and bears the name of the distinguished chief of the Sacs and Foxes. At our first visit there, in 1832, there was a long row of one-story buildings fronting on the river, that were used by Col. Farnham, agent of the American Fur Company, as a store and warehouse—this being the principal depot for trade with the Sacs and Foxes, who were then the sole proprietors of the country and its principal inhabitants, with the exception of a few individuals who had got permission to put up shanties for occupation during the low-water season, while they were engaged in lighting steamers passing up and down the river, but unable to cross the rapids while loaded.

At that day the old chief, Keokuk, boasted of having the handsomest site for a big village that could be found on the river, and since that day it has grown to be a large and elegant city, with wide streets, fine public buildings, nice churches, school-houses, elegant residences, extensive business houses, wholesale and retail stores, manufactories, and a flourishing Medical University with elegant buildings, which has been in successful operation for more than twenty years. The United States District Court for Southern Iowa is also located here. The city is well provided with good hotels. The Patterson House, an immense building, five stories high, being chief, which has always ranked as first-class—with a number of hotels of smaller dimensions, but well kept—affording ample accommodation for the thousands of travelers that frequently congregate at this place. The various professions are represented by men of fine ability—some of them of wide reputation. They have two daily papers, *The Gale City,* and *The Constitution*, which are ably conducted.

A fine canal, running the entire length of the Rapids, from Montrose to Keokuk, has been built by the United States, through which steamboats can now pass at any stage of water—but designed more particularly for low water—so that there is no longer any detention to lighten steamboats over the Rapids.

The City of Muscatine, Iowa.

MUSCATINE WAS FIRST SETTLED AS a wood yard by Col. John Vanater, in July, 1834, and was laid out as a town by him in 1836, and called Bloomington. The county was organized in 1837, under the name of Muscatine, and Bloomington made the county seat. The name of the town was changed to correspond with that of the county in 1851. Its population at the last census was 8,294; present population not less than 10,000. Besides being the centre of a large trade in agricultural products, it is extensively engaged in manufacturing lumber, sash, doors and blinds, and possesses numerous large manufactories, oat-meal mills, and the finest marble works in the State. It is also the centering point of a very large wholesale and retail trade. It is situated at the head of the rich Muscatine Island, the garden spot of the Northwest, and is the shipping point for millions of melons and sweet potatoes annually.

Muscatine is a good town, with a good business and good newspapers. The *Journal* and *Tribune* are published daily, semi-weekly and weekly. Hon. John Mahin has been the editor of the *Journal* since 1852, and there is no editor in the State whose service dates further back than his.

The City of Dubuque

SOON AFTER THE CLOSE OF the war and the discharge of the volunteer army, the writer, with some twenty others who had served through the war, formed a company for the purpose of laying out the town of Dubuque. One of their number, Capt. James Craig, being a surveyor, he was selected to survey the lines and lay out the town. About the middle of September, 1832, he started out from Galena with his chain-carriers, stake-drivers, etc., (stakes having been previously sawed and split on an island opposite, all ready for use), and in due time completed the survey.

Blocks fronting the river on three or four streets back were completed, each lot receiving its stakes, whilst those farther back were staked as blocks, and not subdivided. A few of the original proprietors built and took possession at once. Among them were the Messrs. Langworthy, enterprising and energetic young gentlemen, who commenced business as grocers in a small way, with supplies for miners. Their faith was strong that adventurers would come in, and that the time was not far distant when the town would take a start, and in a few years become a populous city. Miners and prospectors soon took possession of claims in the immediate vicinity, and in one instance a claim was made and ore struck within the limits of our survey.

It was well known that the Indians had been in the habit, for many years, of visiting this portion of their country, for the purpose of getting their supplies of lead; hence the supposition of miners, who had long been engaged in prospecting for lead-mining, that lead would be found on this side of the river and in the vicinity of Dubuque. This caused a great rush to the new fields, of hundreds, who expected to strike it rich with less labor and expense. All were aware, however, that under the treaty just made with the Sacs and Foxes by Gen. Scott and Gov. Reynolds, they had no right to enter upon these lands, and stood in daily fear of being ordered off by United States troops. But their numbers steadily increased. At length the long expected order came. Major Davenport, Indian Agent at Rock Island, was ordered to go forward, and, with one company of infantry in two Mackinaw boats, commanded by Lieut. Beach, they landed near the mouth of Fever river (Galena) about the first of October. The Major came up to Galena with a letter from Col. George Davenport to the writer, to assist him in the discharge of his delicate duty. Word was sent to Lieut. Beach not to proceed up the river until the afternoon of the next day, as the sight of troops by the miners might make them hard to manage; otherwise, I assured the Major, he would have no trouble. We proceeded at once to a point opposite Dubuque, where we found a comfortable stopping place with the ferryman, and he being a man of considerable influence, I suggested to him the propriety of going over to Dubuque to send men to all the mining camps, requesting a meeting the next morning, at nine o'clock, of all the miners, with the agent, to hear what he had to say, and to assure them at the same time that his mission was a peaceable one, and that there should be no objection manifested to disobey the orders of the Government.

After the departure of our messenger we took a private room to talk over the programme for the meeting, when we suggested that, on assembling, the Major should make a little speech explanatory of his visit, in which he should express sorrow for the hardships it would be to leave their claims, with the hope that the time was not distant when all might lawfully return, etc. The Major said he was not a speech-maker, or a very good talker, but would read the orders sent to him to dispossess them, and see that they crossed the river.

After some discussion, the writer, at his request, wrote out a short address for the Major, and on going over the next morning, we met some four or five hundred miners at the grocery store, who had assembled to listen to the orders sent for their removal. There being no boards or boxes into which to improvise a stand for the speaker, a whisky-barrel was introduced, from the head of which, after apologizing to the miners for the disagreeable duty that had been placed upon the Major, and in consequence of his suffering from a bad cold, we had taken the stand to read to them his short address, and as most of them had spent the summer in the service of the Government as soldiers in the field, and had been honorably discharged, the Major felt satisfied that there would be no objection manifested by anyone in the large crowd before us to disobey an order from the Government. After the close of the Major's address, the question was put to vote by raising of hands. There was a general upraising of hands, which was declared to be unanimous for immediate removal. Owing to the good treatment received by the Major, he proposed to treat the entire party, and, to facilitate the matter, buckets of whisky with tin cups were passed around, and after all had partaken they shook hands with the Major and commenced Crossing over in flatboats.

At three o'clock in the afternoon we crossed over on the last boat, and took our departure for Galena. During the evening the Major's report of how his peaceable removal of a large body of intruders from the west to the east bank of the Mississippi had been accomplished, was made out and mailed. But the further fact that all those miners had recrossed the river, and were then in their mining camps, was not recorded, for the reason that the Major had not been posted as to their intentions.

Owing to the provisions of the treaty, it was a long time before Congress passed an act for the sale of these lands, and confirmation to the titles of town sites, hence, many of those who had laid out the town of Dubuque had left the county, and at the time of proving up their claims failed to put in an appearance—the writer being one of them—whilst those who remained, with the Messrs. Langworthy, became sole proprietors—the latter having lived to see the town rise in importance, and at this time become one of the most populous cities on the west side of the Mississippi.

A Note About the Author

Sauk Chief Black Hawk (1767–1838) was a chief of the Sauk Native American tribe. Born Ma-ka-tai-me-she-kia-kiak in Saukenuk, a village along the Rock River, Black Hawk was the son of medicine man Pyesa and a descendant of Chief Nanamakee. He found success as a young warrior on raids with his father, eventually leading a group of 200 men against the rival Osage. Following Pyesa's death in battle with the Cherokee, Black Hawk inherited his father's medicine bundle and took on a leadership role in the tribe. During the War of 1812, he fought alongside the British against American forces, hoping to regain Sauk territory stolen by white settlers. In 1832, Black Hawk, backed by his so-called British Band of warriors from several tribes, declared war against the Michigan and Illinois Territories. Waged between April and August 1832, the Black Hawk War ended with the chief's surrender to Lieutenant Jefferson Davis, who would go on to lead the Confederacy during the Civil War. Released after nearly a year in captivity, Black Hawk dictated his life story to government interpreter Antoine LeClair. The *Autobiography of Ma-Ka-Tai-Me-She-Kia-Kiak* (1833) was published in Cincinatti, making Black Hawk the first Native American to have an autobiography appear in print.

A Note from the Publisher

Spanning many genres, from non-fiction essays to literature classics to children's books and lyric poetry, Mint Edition books showcase the master works of our time in a modern new package. The text is freshly typeset, is clean and easy to read, and features a new note about the author in each volume. Many books also include exclusive new introductory material. Every book boasts a striking new cover, which makes it as appropriate for collecting as it is for gift giving. Mint Edition books are only printed when a reader orders them, so natural resources are not wasted. We're proud that our books are never manufactured in excess and exist only in the exact quantity they need to be read and enjoyed.

bookfinity™

Discover more of your favorite classics with Bookfinity™.

- Track your reading with custom book lists.
- Get great book recommendations for your personalized Reader Type.
- Add reviews for your favorite books.
- AND MUCH MORE!

Visit **bookfinity.com** and take the fun Reader Type quiz to get started.

Enjoy our classic and modern companion pairings!